Name ....زكريا وهر تذبير..........

Class ....

Teacher ....

Madrasah ....

Muhammad Qasim Qadri Ridwi
Imam Khateeb & Teacher
07534 895 335
sunnihanafi@hotmail.com

14-9-2021

Qamar Islamic Studies Level Three

Second edition, 2017

Part of the Qamar Islamic Studies series

Published by

Qamar Learning Academy, Bolton, England

admin@qamarislamicstudies.org

Edited by

Mohsin Adam Haveliwala

Cover design by

Maksud Yusuf

Designed and created by Qamar Learning Academy in the UK. 🇬🇧

ISBN: 978-1-9997906-2-2

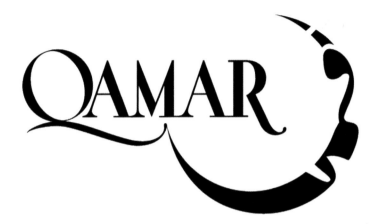

Qamar Learning Academy

Preface

All praise belongs to Allah ﷻ most high, who guided us to Islam, gave us the opportunity to seek His pleasure through serving the faith and strengthened us through His immense generosity.

Let the loftiest of salutations be showered upon our Liege Lord Muhammad ﷺ, his family, companions and all those who follow his way.

Following on from the success of the first edition of Qamar Islamic Studies in 2016, many scholars, teachers, institutes, madrasas and mosques demanded that the team continue to build upon the first three books. The team of students who dedicated so many sincere hours to the cause came together again to deliver a new, updated and broader second edition along with book 4 of the series.

Qamar Academy's aim is to try and enhance the learning experience for children across the UK and we have sought to further our aims through the changes made since the first edition was published. We ask Allah to grant us sincerity, accept our meagre efforts and help us to aid young Muslims in their learning journey.

I would like to thank all those who have helped us once again and I look forward to working with the brothers and sisters who will, if Allah wills, help us in the future.

We accept that we will fall short of perfection. If you find any errors in this work then please write to us on the e-mail address on the inside cover of the book.

We ask Allah for success.

Mohsin Adam Haveliwala

July 4th 2017, 8 Shawwal 1438

The Role of Parents

It is amazing to see the position that Allah ﷻ has granted us in this life. He has made us parents but also guardians of children who will form a part of the future of this world.

Our fate in this world and the next is tied to the fate of our children. As a parent, it is easy to be overwhelmed by the level of responsibility we carry in this regard. There are some simple steps that we can take, as well as things we can think about, in order to ensure that we facilitate a positive learning journey for our children. It is worth reflecting on some of these mentioned below.

1. The eyes and ears of children are the entry points into their souls. Whatever enters their souls from the eyes or ears will have some impact on their spiritual and intellectual wellbeing. It is best to be wary and protect their souls adequately.

2. The most significant teaching relationship children have is with their parents. If they see certain actions and hear certain words from their parents, they will immediately be driven towards accepting them.

3. Good quality learning at home is far more powerful for a child's development than any classroom-based activities.

4. Regularly talking with children about what they have learnt will enhance their learning experience and increase the level of benefit they attain.

5. It is best to allocate a certain time once or twice a week to review the content of a child's learning journey. Only then can we be confident of understanding their progress.

6. Reading to your child regularly is very important for the reinforcement of a learning message.

7. Listen to your child reading regularly.

8. Ask your child to read to you and to tell you the stories that they have learned.

9. Set an expectation with your child each week and map the journey on a wall poster so that they know what to aim for.

10. Rewarding children's achievements will ensure that they enjoy a positive learning experience.

11. Ask Allah ﷻ for success in their learning as all matters are for His pleasure.
    Finally, you can ensure that your child's learning is advanced through their everyday life by helping them to complete actions in line with the Qur'aan and Sunnah. Helping them perform wudhu, ghusl, helping them to eat, drink and interact with others in an Islamic manner. This can be further enhanced through sound discipline by limiting time with a TV, computer games, excessive socialisation and music.

We ask Allah ﷻ for success on behalf of our children, ourselves and all people everywhere.

Contents

AQIDAH

Lesson One-Belief in Allah   11

Lesson Two-Prophets of Allah   13

Lesson Three-Books of Allah   15

Lesson Four-Companions of the Prophet   19

Lesson Five-Loving the Prophet Muhammad   21

Lesson Six-Family of Prophet Muhammad   25

Lesson Seven-The grave   27

Lesson Eight-The Day of Judgement   29

FIQH (HANAFI)

Revision from Level two   33

Lesson One-Makrooh acts of Wudhu   37

Lesson Two-Mustahab acts of Wudhu   39

Lesson Three-Ghusl   41

Lesson Four-Tayammum   45

Lesson Five-Conditions for Tayammum   49

Lesson Six-Faraidh of Salah   51

Lesson Seven-Salah chart   53

Lesson Eight-Virtues of Salah   57

Lesson Nine-Method of performing Salah   59

 *Jalla Jalaluhu.* May his glory be exalted.

 Sallallahu Alayhi Wa Sallam. Allah bless him and grant him peace.

 Alayhis Salaam. Peace be upon him.

HISTORY

Lesson One-Arabia — 67

Lesson Two-The Quraysh and Arabs — 69

Lesson Three-The Holy Ka'bah — 71

Lesson Four-Birth of our Prophet Muhammad ﷺ — 75

Lesson Five-Life in the desert — 77

Lesson Six-Childhood — 81

Lesson Seven-Journey to Al-Shaam — 83

Lesson Eight-Second trip to Al-Shaam — 87

Lesson Nine-The marriage — 89

Lesson Ten- Rebuilding of the Holy Ka'bah — 91

Lesson Eleven-First revelation — 95

Lesson Twelve-Islamic movement — 99

Lesson Thirteen-Torture and persecution — 101

Lesson Fourteen-Year of Sorrow — 105

Lesson Fifteen-Meraj Un Nabi — 107

Lesson Sixteen-First Pledge of Aqaba — 111

AKHLAQ

Lesson One-Reciting the Qur'aan — 117

Lesson Two-The Masjid — 121

Lesson Three-Prophetic Character — 125

Lesson Four-Manners of eating and drinking — 127

Lesson Five-Walking — 129

Lesson Six-Talking to others — 131

Lesson Seven-Valuing your time — 127

Lesson Eight-Giving gifts — 129

Lesson Nine-Honouring our neighbours — 131

Radi Allahu Anhu. May Allah be pleased with him.

Radi Allahu Anha. May Allah be pleased with her.

Radi Allahu Anhuma. May Allah be pleased with them both.

بِسْمِ اللهِ الرَّحْمَنِ الرَّحِيمِ

الْحَمْدُ لِلّهِ رَبِّ الْعَالَمِينَ

وَصَلَّى اللهُ عَلَى سَيِّدِنَا مُحَمَّدٍ وَّعَلَى آلِهِ وَصَحْبِهِ أَجْمَعِينَ

نَوَيْتُ التَّعَلُّمَ وَالتَّعْلِيمَ وَالتَّذَكُّرَ وَالتَّذْكِيرَ وَالنَّفْعَ وَالإِنْتِفَاعَ
وَالإِفَادَةَ وَالإِسْتِفَادَةَ وَالْحَثَّ عَلَى التَّمَسُّكِ بِكِتَابِ اللهِ وَسُنَّةِ
رَسُولِهِ وَالدُّعَاءَ إِلَى الْهُدَى وَالدَّلَالَةَ عَلَى الْخَيْرِ وَابْتِغَاءَ وَجْهِ اللهِ
وَمَرْضَاتِهِ وَقُرْبِهِ وَثَوَابِهِ سُبْحَانَهُ وَتَعَالَى

In the name of Allah ﷻ, the Entirely Merciful, the Especially Merciful

All praise to Allah ﷻ, Lord of the Worlds

And salutations and greetings upon our master Muhammad ﷺ and upon his family and companions

I intend to study and teach, take and give a reminder, take and give benefit, take and give advantage, to encourage the holding fast to the book of Allah ﷻ and the way of His Messenger ﷺ, and calling to guidance and directing towards good, hoping for the countenance of Allah ﷻ and His pleasure, proximity and reward, transcendent is He.

Qamar Learning Academy

اَلعَقِيدَة

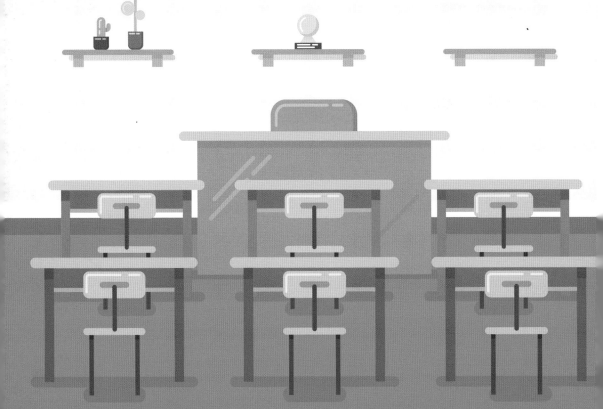

What's in this section?

BELIEF IN ALLAH (ﷻ)

PROPHETS OF ALLAH (ﷻ)

BOOKS OF ALLAH (ﷻ)

- Holy Qur'aan

COMPANIONS OF PROPHET MUHAMMAD (ﷺ)

LOVING THE PROPHET MUHAMMAD (ﷺ)

THE PROPHET MUHAMMAD'S (ﷺ) **FAMILY**

THE GRAVE

THE DAY OF JUDGEMENT

AQIDAH

Allah ﷻ is one, pure and free from all faults. He is the only one worthy of worship. He has no beginning nor does He have an end; He will remain forever. He has no partner. Neither is Allah ﷻ the father or son of anyone nor does He have a spouse. Whoever believes that Allah ﷻ is the father or son of anyone or believes that Allah ﷻ has a spouse, is a disbeliever.

Everything other than Allah ﷻ is created. The universe and all its parts have been created by Allah ﷻ. The Earth, sky, moon, stars and the sun are all the creations of Allah ﷻ.

Allah ﷻ is "Hayy". This means He is self-existing. The lives of everyone and everything is in his control. He gives life to whomsoever He wills and causes death whenever He wills.

Allah ﷻ is free from a body, shape or form. He does not eat or drink, nor does He sleep. Nothing is like Allah ﷻ.

Allah ﷻ is not dependent on anyone or anything. He is free from all types of need. Rather, the entire universe is dependent on Allah ﷻ.

Allah ﷻ is all knowing. He knows every single thing and His knowledge has no limit. Allah ﷻ knows the secrets and what is more deeply hidden. There is nothing that he is unaware of.

EXERCISE ONE

COMPLETE THE WORDSEARCH. AN EXAMPLE IS SHOWN BELOW.

```
W I H T C H C M Z B R O A
Y J S E R Z A O R Y G T D
U X L M S E R O N N N Z A
T A S A I O E N L G Z X R
T U X Y T F M S V D F D L
N S H A R S O D F C S A A
O Z E R Z I A L Z L N T Y
B R N R T G G T R C C J W
C E A R T H X R U G T J F
P E C J U H B Q L Z F S U
L N Z R Y T N Y W H F X X
P F I R M L K J T P C X J
H Y K S U C M H Y D Y L K
```

Sun	Creator
~~Earth~~	Moon
Trees	Sky

1. Prophets عليهم السلام are special servants of Allah who have been sent to guide people to the right path.

2. All Prophets عليهم السلام are male. There have been no female Prophets.

3. One cannot become a Prophet through worship and effort, rather every Prophet is chosen by Allah.

4. Prophets عليهم السلام cannot sin.

5. Prophets عليهم السلام always perform good deeds.

6. Prophets عليهم السلام are faultless. No one should ever speak badly of them.

7. Muslims must believe in all the Prophets عليهم السلام.

8. Prophets عليهم السلام are blessed with the most excellent of qualities like truthfulness (Sidq), intelligence (Fatanah), trustworthiness (Amanah), beauty and wisdom.

8. We must respect all Prophets عليهم السلام.

9. Our Prophet Muhammad has the highest position amongst all the Prophets عليهم السلام.

10. The one who rejects even one Prophet of Allah عليه السلام is not a believer.

EXERCISE TWO

Right Path	Respect	Worship
Highest	Faultless	Sin

1. We must _____ all Prophets عليهم السلام who came into this world.

2. Prophets عليهم السلام are _____.

3. One who is sent to guide people to the _____ _____ is a Prophet.

4. Our Prophet Muhammad ﷺ has the _____ position amongst all the Prophets.

5. One cannot be a Prophet due to _____ or effort.

6. Prophets عليهم السلام cannot _____.

1. Allah ﷻ sent down many books from the time of Sayyiduna Adam عليه السلام to the time of Prophet Muhammad ﷺ.

2. These books were sent to help people worship and recognise Allah ﷻ.

3. There are 4 main books which were revealed. They are **Zaboor**, **Torah**, **Injeel** and the **Holy Qur'aan**.

4. **Zaboor** was revealed to Sayyiduna Dawood عليه السلام. He was given the ability to speak to the birds and the birds would sing along with him. He was also a great king and judge. He is a messenger of Allah ﷻ and the father of Sayyiduna Sulayman عليه السلام.

5. The **Torah** was revealed to Sayyiduna Musa عليه السلام. He is a messenger of Allah ﷻ. He was sent to the nation of Bani Israeel. Allah ﷻ gave him miracles when faced with the Pharaoh's magicians. He had a stick which turned into a large snake when he threw it down.

6. **Injeel** was revealed to Sayyiduna Isa عليه السلام. He is a messenger of Allah ﷻ and he was born without a father. His mother's name is Sayyida Maryam رضي الله عنها. Allah ﷻ gave him the ability to cure those who were blind from birth as well as being able to raise the dead through Allah's ﷻ will.

7. The **Holy Qur'aan** was revealed to our Prophet Muhammad ﷺ. He is the last messenger to come into this world. He was sent as a guide for all creation. The Prophet Muhammad ﷺ is the greatest of all creation and He is the beloved of Allah ﷻ.

THE HOLY QUR'AAN

- The Holy Qur'aan is the final and most perfect book sent down upon the Messenger of Allah ﷺ through angel Jibreel ﷺ

- The revelation of the Holy Qur'aan began in the holy month of Ramadaan after Our Prophet Muhammad ﷺ passed the 40th year of his blessed life in the cave of Hira.

- The first revelation sent upon our Prophet Muhammad ﷺ was the first few verses of Surah Al-Alaq.

- The Holy Qur'aan was not revealed all at once but in phases over a total of 23 years.

- It is compulsory to believe in all the chapters of the Holy Qur'aan.

- The Holy Qur'aan is the word of Allah ﷻ. We should therefore treat it with respect.

- The Holy Qur'aan is a sacred book. No one may touch it unless they have Wudhu.

- The Holy Qur'aan is a universal book which Allah ﷻ took upon Himself to preserve. It's text has never been changed, not even a single syllable or a word, since it was revealed. It will remain unchanged until the end of time.

1. There were _____ famous books revealed by Allah ⓖ.

2. The names of the famous books are:

_____

_____

3. _____ was revealed to Sayyiduna Dawood ⓔ.

4. _____ was revealed to Sayyiduna Musa ⓔ.

5. _____ was revealed to Sayyiduna Isa ⓔ.

6. _____ was revealed to Sayyiduna Muhammad ⓢ.

1. A Sahabi (companion) is a person who saw the Prophet Muhammad ﷺ in the state of Imaan (faith) and passed away in the state of Imaan.

2. All companions are noble and honest.

3. All companions are highly honoured and respected.

4. The most honoured Sahabi is the honourable Sayyiduna Abu Bakr Al-Siddiq ﵁. His real name is Abdullah Bin Abi Quhafah ﵁.

5. Anyone who speaks ill about any Sahabi will be sinful. This is because our Prophet Muhammad ﷺ did not allow this. He said, "Whenever you find someone speaking ill about my companions, say to him, may Allah's ﷻ curse be upon you".

6. Companions are guides for Muslims. Our Prophet ﷺ says, "My companions are like the stars. Whoever among them you use for guidance, you will be rightly guided".

7. All the companions of our Prophet ﷺ will enter Jannah and have a high status.

8. All the companions of the Prophet ﷺ are good and fair people.

9. When we mention a companion of the Prophet ﷺ it must be done with respect.

10. Sayyiduna Abu Bakr Al-Siddiq ﵁ was the first male to accept Islam; the first woman to accept Islam was Sayyida Khadija ﵂ and from amongst the children, Sayyiduna Ali ﵁ was the first to accept Islam.

EXERCISE FOUR

TICK TRUE OR FALSE FOR THE FOLLOWING STATEMENTS.

	True	False
1. All the companions of the Prophet ﷺ will enter Jannah.	☐	☐
2. Some companions are religious and honest.	☐	☐
3. A Sahabi is a person who saw the Prophet ﷺ with Imaan.	☐	☐
4. From all children, Sayyiduna Ali ؓ was the first to accept Islam.	☐	☐
5. Anyone who speaks ill about a companion will not be sinful.	☐	☐

1. Loving the Prophet ﷺ is the root of Imaan. Our Imaan is complete when we love our Prophet ﷺ more than anything and everything in this world.

2. The Prophet ﷺ said, "None of you truly believes until I am dearer to him than his children, his parents and all people".

3. The Prophet ﷺ is the most beloved to Allah ﷻ. That's why he is the greatest of creation in the world and the Leader of all Prophets عليهم السلام.

4. Loving the Prophet ﷺ is also a proof of loving Allah ﷻ. Allah ﷻ says, "O Prophet ﷺ you say, if you truly love Allah ﷻ then follow me. Allah ﷻ will love you and forgive your sins. Allah ﷻ is the Most Forgiving, All Merciful".

5. To show love for the Prophet ﷺ, we must follow his teachings and guidance.

6. We must express our love for the Prophet ﷺ by sending blessings and salutations (Durood) upon him. Sending blessings and salutations is an act commanded by Allah ﷻ. Even Allah ﷻ and his angels send blessings upon Sayyiduna Muhammad ﷺ.

7. One of the signs of love for the Prophet ﷺ is to love the family of the Prophet ﷺ. Our Prophet ﷺ says, "My family (Ahl-ul-Bait) is like the ark of Nuh عليه السلام, whoever gets on the boat is saved and whoever does not is destroyed."

8. Another sign of love for the Prophet ﷺ is to love all the companions of the Prophet ﷺ.

9. Yet another sign of love for the Prophet ﷺ is to remember him in different ways such as learning about his life, his habits, his manners and praising him in the way that the companions and pious scholars have done.

10. We must respect all objects connected to the Prophet ﷺ such as the blessed hair as well as his belongings, which can still be seen today.

Al-Salaat Al-Ibrahimi

اللّٰهُمَّ صَلِّ عَلَى مُحَمَّدٍ وَّعَلَى آلِ مُحَمَّدٍ، كَمَا صَلَّيْتَ عَلَى إِبْرَاهِيمَ وَعَلَى آلِ إِبْرَاهِيمَ، إِنَّكَ حَمِيدٌ مَجِيدٌ، اللّٰهُمَّ بَارِكْ عَلَى مُحَمَّدٍ، وَّعَلَى آلِ مُحَمَّدٍ، كَمَا بَارَكْتَ عَلَى إِبْرَاهِيمَ، وَعَلَى آلِ إِبْرَاهِيمَ، إِنَّكَ حَمِيدٌ مَجِيدٌ

EXERCISE FIVE

FILL IN THE GAPS USING THE WORDS IN THE BOXES BELOW.

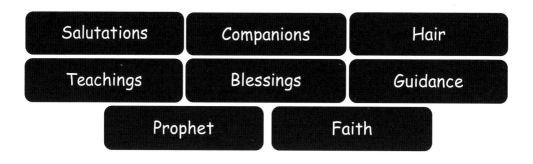

Salutations	Companions	Hair
Teachings	Blessings	Guidance
Prophet	Faith	

1. To show our love for the Prophet ﷺ, we must follow his _____ and _____.

2. We must express our love for the Prophet ﷺ by sending _____ and _____ upon him.

3. Loving the _____ is also a proof of loving Allah ﷻ.

4. We must respect the things connected to the Prophet ﷺ such as the blessed _____ of the Prophet ﷺ.

5. Another sign of love for the Prophet ﷺ is to love the _____ of the Prophet ﷺ.

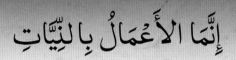

إِنَّمَا الأَعْمَالُ بِالنِّيَّاتِ

Actions are only according to intentions.

(Al-Bukhari)

This hadith explains one of the most important aspects of Islam; sincere intentions in one's worship.

Lessons learnt from this hadith:

- Before, after and whilst doing any actions we should check our intentions.
- We should always do things to please Allah ﷻ alone and only then will Allah ﷻ reward us.
- If Shaytaan spoils our intentions, we should ask for forgiveness from Allah ﷻ and we should correct our intentions.
- We should learn to work with others with sincerity and without any expectation of any favours in return.

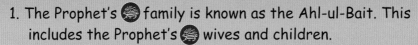

LESSON SIX-THE PROPHET MUHAMMAD'S ﷺ FAMILY

1. The Prophet's ﷺ family is known as the Ahl-ul-Bait. This includes the Prophet's ﷺ wives and children.

2. The Prophet Muhammad ﷺ had 3 sons; Sayyiduna Qasim ؓ, Sayyiduna Abdullah ؓ and Sayyiduna Ibrahim ؓ.

3. Our Prophet Muhammad ﷺ had 4 daughters;

   -Sayyida Ruqayya ؓ

   -Sayyida Umm Kulthum ؓ

   -Sayyida Zainab ؓ

   -Sayyida Fatima ؓ

4. The grandsons of the Prophet ﷺ are Imam Hasan ؓ and Imam Hussain ؓ. Their children are also part of the Ahl-ul-Bait.

5. Sayyiduna Ali ؓ was the fourth Khalifa of Islam and the cousin of our Prophet Muhammad ﷺ.

6. The Prophet ﷺ had 11 wives.

7. To love the Ahl-ul-Bait is to love the Prophet ﷺ.

8. The love of the Ahl-ul-Bait will help us to be successful on the Day of Judgement.

9. The Prophet ﷺ is reported to have said, "*Love for the Ahl-ul-Bait will help one to cross the Siraat (bridge) safely on the Day of Judgement.*"

10. To love the Ahl-ul-Bait is an important aspect of our Aqidah (Faith). We must love them, respect them and assist them.

EXERCISE SIX

1. Name the grandsons of our Prophet 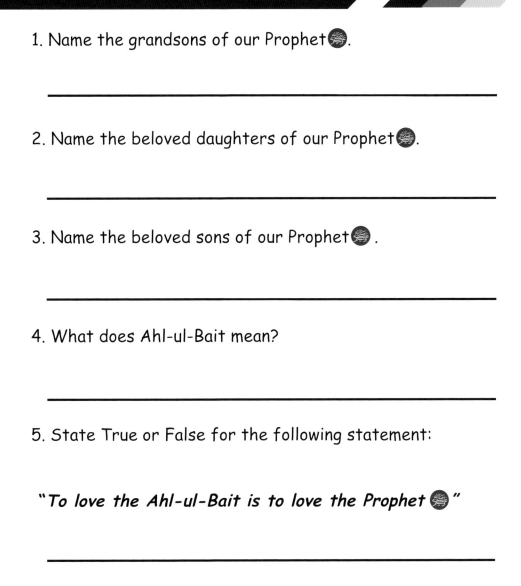.

_____

2. Name the beloved daughters of our Prophet.

_____

3. Name the beloved sons of our Prophet.

_____

4. What does Ahl-ul-Bait mean?

_____

5. State True or False for the following statement:

"To love the Ahl-ul-Bait is to love the Prophet "

_____

LESSON SEVEN-THE GRAVE

1. When Muslims die, they are buried in a grave.

مَنْ رَّبُّكَ؟

2. In the grave, a person will be awoken so that they can be questioned.

3. Two Angels, named Munkar and Nakeer, are sent to the grave to ask three questions.

مَا دِيْنُكَ؟

4. The first question is

   "Who is your Lord?"

5. The second question is

   "What is your religion?"

6. The third question is

   "What did you say about this man? (The Prophet Muhammad ﷺ)

7. Those who answer the questions correctly will find comfort in their grave.

مَا كُنْتَ تَقُوْلُ فِي هَذَا الرَّجُلِ؟

8. Those who answer the questions incorrectly will find discomfort and punishment in their graves.

9. To answer the questions correctly, we must practise our religion in this life.

10. People will stay in their graves until the Day of Judgement.

COLOUR IN THE CORRECT BLOCK AND COMPLETE THE SENTENCES BELOW.

1) The questions in the grave are asked by...

MUNKAR & NAKEER	KIRAMAN & KATIBEEN	ANGEL JIBRAEEL

2) When Muslims die they are...

BURIED IN A SEA	BURIED IN A CAR	BURIED IN A GRAVE

3) If the questions are answered incorrectly, graves will become...

LONGER	BRIGHTER	UNCOMFORTABLE

4) If the questions are answered correctly, graves will become...

UNCOMFORTABLE	DARKER	COMFORTABLE

5) The total number of questions that will be asked in the grave is...

FIVE	THREE	FOUR

LESSON EIGHT-THE DAY OF JUDGEMENT يَوُمُ الْقِيَامَةِ

1. The Day of Judgement is a day when all humans and Jinn will stand before Allah ﷻ to answer for their deeds.

2. On that day, people will be reminded about their deeds when they were still alive in this world.

3. It is a day when people will be so scared that they will not even recognise their own family.

4. Those who committed bad deeds during their lives will be punished with Jahannam (Hell) by the justice of Allah ﷻ.

5. Those who committed good deeds during their lives will be rewarded with Jannah (Paradise) by the mercy of Allah ﷻ.

6. The day will be 50,000 years long.

7. The sun will be a mile above a person's head.

8. People will sweat according to the amount of bad deeds in their life. Some will sweat up to their ankles, some up to their knees and some will drown in their own sweat.

9. Those who lived their lives as good Muslims will have no fear on that day. They will be treated with respect.

10. Our Prophet Muhammad ﷺ will help his followers by interceding for them with Allah ﷻ and asking Allah ﷻ to forgive them.

EXERCISE EIGHT

DRAW LINES BETWEEN THE BOXES TO MAKE COMPLETE SENTENCES.

The Day of Judgement	Result in Jahannam
Good deeds can	Fear on this day
Bad deeds can	Will be 50,000 years long
There will be a lot of	Result in Jannah

NOW HAVE A GO AT MAKING YOUR OWN SENTENCES AND TEST YOUR FRIEND

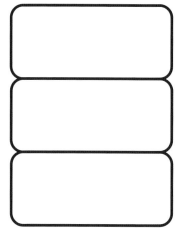

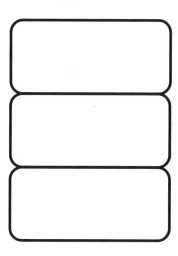

Qamar Learning Academy

اَلْفِقُه

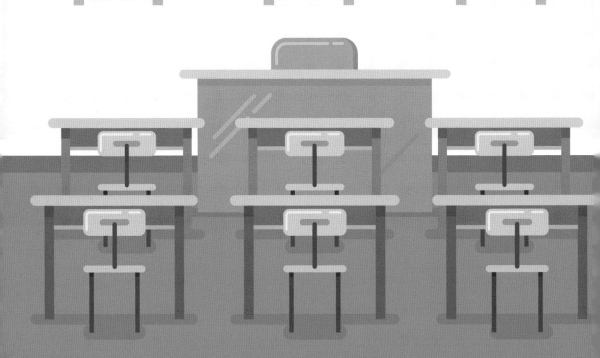

What's in this section?

REVISION FROM LEVEL TWO

MAKROOH ACTS OF WUDHU

MUSTAHAB ACTS OF WUDHU

GHUSL
- Method of Ghusl

TAYAMMUM
- Faraidh of Tayammum

CONDITIONS FOR TAYAMMUM

FARAIDH OF SALAH

SALAH CHART

VIRTUES OF SALAH

METHOD OF PERFORMING SALAH
- Model prayer

FIQH

Fiqh Terms

Fardh فرض: An act that is obligatory, so it must be performed.

Wajib واجب: An act that is necessary and it is almost as important as a Fardh act.

Sunnah سنة: An action which our Prophet Muhammad ﷺ has done or liked.

Mustahab مستحب: An act which is liked and if you do it, you get reward.

Haram حَرَام: An act which is forbidden.

Makrooh مكروه: An act which is disliked.

The Faraidh of Wudhu

1. To wash the full face from the start of the forehead, where the hair begins to grow to the bottom of the chin and from one earlobe to the other once.

2. To wash both arms including the elbows at least once.

3. To perform Masah. This means to wet both hands once and wipe at least a quarter of the head at least once.

4. To wash both feet, including the ankles, at least once.

The practical method of Wudhu

1. Make Niyyah (intention).

2. Recite Tasmiyah.

3. Wash the hands, including the wrists, three times.

4. Wash our mouth three times and clean our teeth. If possible, it is best to use a Miswak to clean our teeth.

5. Wash the nostrils three times using our right hand and clean the nose using the left hand.

6. We then wash our face three times.

7. Wash both our arms, including the elbows, three times.

8. Wipe our whole head (Masah) using wet hands.

9. Wash both of our feet and make Khilaal of our toes.

10. Recite the Duaa after Wudhu.

What breaks Wudhu?

1. The passing of urine, stool or the passing of wind.

2. Vomiting a mouthful.

3. Flowing blood or pus.

4. Sleeping.

5. Fainting

6. Laughing loudly in Salah.

7. When there is more blood than saliva in the mouth.

8. Being drunk.

REVISION FROM LEVEL TWO

What are the Faraidh of Ghusl?

1. To wash the mouth and gargle.

2. To put water in the nose and clean up to the top of the nostrils.

3. To pour water over the entire body from head to toe without leaving any part dry.

Method of making Ghusl

1. Make Niyyah (Intention).

2. Wash both hands up to the wrist.

3. Wash the private parts.

4. Perform Wudhu.

5. Pour water over the head three times.

6. Pour water over the right shoulder three times.

7. Pour water over the left shoulder three times.

8. Scrub the body properly as water is poured so that no part of the body is left dry.

Adhaan and Iqamah

1. It is Sunnah to call the Adhaan to invite people to prayer.

2. The Muadhin must face the Qiblah when calling the Adhaan.

3. It is Sunnah to call out the Adhaan in the state of Wudhu.

4. Adhaan should be called out after the time of Salah begins.

5. Adhaan should be given in a loud voice.

6. Iqamah is called before the beginning of the Jama'ah Salah.

7. The one who gives the Iqamah is called a Mukabbir.

8. Iqamah is given in a soft voice but loud enough so that those in the mosque can hear it.

Conditions of Salah

1. Our clothes must be clean and pure.

2. Our body must be covered.

3. The place of Salah where we pray must be clean.

4. Our body must be clean and pure.

5. We must pray Salah at the correct time.

6. We must face the Qiblah.

7. We must make Niyyah before performing Salah.

8. We must recite Allahu Akbar to start our Salah.

LESSON ONE-MAKROOH ACTS OF WUDHU

THERE ARE CERTAIN ACTIONS WHICH ARE DISLIKED (MAKROOH) WHEN PERFORMING WUDHU. THESE ACTIONS DECREASE THE REWARD OF WUDHU AND BLESSINGS ARE LOST. WE SHOULD AVOID THESE ACTIONS BECAUSE THEY ARE NOT LIKED BY ALLAH ﷻ.

Which actions are Makrooh in Wudhu?

To clean the nose with our right hand. We should always try and use the left hand to clean our nose.

To use more water than needed. We should not waste water.

To perform Wudhu in a dirty place. We should perform Wudhu in a clean place.

To talk about worldly affairs during Wudhu. It is better not to talk during Wudhu.

To wash our face with one hand. We should wash our face using both hands.

EXERCISE ONE

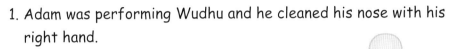

HELP THESE PEOPLE UNDERSTAND WHETHER THEY HAVE PERFORMED A MAKROOH ACT OR NOT.

1. Adam was performing Wudhu and he cleaned his nose with his right hand.

   Did he perform a Makrooh act?

   Yes   No

2. Salma was performing Wudhu and she washed her face with two hands.

   Did she perform a Makrooh act?

   Yes   No

   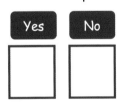

3. Yusuf was performing Wudhu in a dirty place.

   Did he perform a Makrooh act?

   Yes   No

   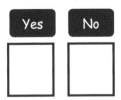

WHEN MAKING WUDHU, THERE ARE CERTAIN ACTS THAT ARE PREFERABLE (MUSTAHAB). IF YOU PERFORM THEM, YOU WILL GAIN REWARD AND IF YOU LEAVE THEM THERE IS NO SIN. WUDHU WILL STILL BE VALID. PERFORMING THESE ACTS SHOWS LOVE FOR ALLAH ﷻ AND HIS MESSENGER ﷺ.

What are the Mustahab acts of Wudhu?

To face the Qiblah.

To make Wudhu in a clean place.

To read Tasmiyah before washing each part.

بِسْمِ اللَّهِ الرَّحْمَنِ الرَّحِيمِ

To begin with the right when washing each part of Wudhu.

To clean the nose with the left hand.

EXERCISE TWO

To make Wudhu in a clean place. ☐	To clean the nose with the left hand. ☐
To clean the nose with the right hand. ☐	To perform Masah of the whole head. ☐
To read Tasmiyah before washing each part. ☐	To wash and gargle the mouth. ☐
To wash the face with one hand. ☐	To face the Qiblah. ☐
To begin with the right when washing each part of Wudhu. ☐	To make Niyyah. ☐

GHUSL MEANS TO HAVE A BATH. WE SHOULD PERFORM GHUSL REGULARLY. OUR PROPHET MUHAMMAD ﷺ USED TO HAVE A BATH REGULARLY, ESPECIALLY BEFORE THE JUMUAH PRAYER. ALLAH ﷻ LOVES THOSE WHO ARE CLEAN. CLEANLINESS IS A VERY IMPORTANT PART OF OUR FAITH.

The Faraidh of Ghusl (Mentioned before)

1. Rinse the entire mouth.

2. To put water in the nose and clean up to the top of the nostrils.

3. Pour water over the whole body, from head to toe, without leaving a single hair dry.

Ghusl will not be complete if any of the Faraidh are left out or are incomplete.

The following are important to remember

1. To wash the inside of the navel.
2. To wet the roots of the hair.
3. To wash the inner part of the nose.
4. To wash under the armpits.
5. To wash behind the knees.
6. To wash the inner part of the ears and ear piercing.

METHOD OF GHUSL

1. Make the intention for Ghusl.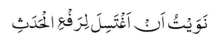

2. Wash both hands three times up to the wrist.

3. Wash the private parts thoroughly.

4. All dirt from the body should be removed.

5. Perform Wudhu.

6. Pour water over the right shoulder three times and left shoulder three times.

7. Pour water over the head and the whole body three times.

8. Wash the feet when Ghusl is completed and then leave the place of Ghusl.

9. Make Ghusl in a private place. If you are making Ghusl in the bathroom, make sure the door is closed.

10. Make sure you do not read or speak while making Ghusl. If somebody calls you and you need to reply, then make a noise or sound like you are clearing your throat. The person will know that you are making Ghusl and will not disturb you.

11. Dry the body with a clean towel or cloth.

EXERCISE THREE

LIST THE THREE FARAIDH OF GHUSL IN THE CORRECT ORDER BELOW.

1._____

_____

_____

2._____

_____

_____

3._____

_____

_____

Feet	Speak	Niyyah	Private	Hands
Dirt	Head	Dry	Wudhu	Read

1. Make the_____ for Ghusl.

2. Wash both of the_____ three times up to the wrist.

3. Wash the private parts thoroughly.

4. All_____ from the body should be removed.

5. Perform _____.

6. Pour water over the right shoulder three times and left shoulder three times.

7. Pour water over the_____ and the whole body three times.

8. Wash the_____ when Ghusl is completed and then leave the place of Ghusl.

9. Make Ghusl in a_____ place.

10. Make sure you do not_____ or_____ while making Ghusl.

11. _____ the body with a clean towel or cloth.

LESSON FOUR-TAYAMMUM

THE MEANING OF TAYAMMUM IS DRY ABLUTION. TAYAMMUM IS A SPECIAL WAY OF PURIFYING OURSELVES. TAYAMMUM CAN BE PERFORMED WITH SAND, STONE OR SOIL WHEN NO WATER IS AVAILABLE. TAYAMMUM IS LIKE WUDHU AS IT ENABLES US TO PRAY SALAH OR TOUCH THE QUR'AAN.

How do we perform Tayammum?

1. Make intention to perform Tayammum like Wudhu or Ghusl.

2. Strike both hands on clean earth like sand or soil.

3. Pass the hands over the face.

4. Once again, strike both hands on clean earth like sand or soil.

5. Wipe the arms including the elbows.

FARAIDH OF TAYAMMUM

1. To make intention for Tayammum.

2. To wipe your hands all over the face without leaving any part untouched.

3. To wipe your hands over both arms including the elbows.

NUMBER THESE PICTURES FROM 1-5 IN THE CORRECT ORDER BELOW.

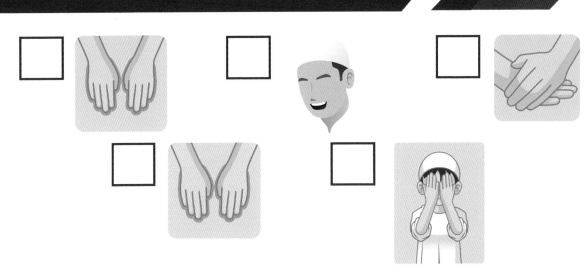

NOW THAT YOU KNOW WHAT IS INVOLVED IN TAYAMMUM, FIND A SUITABLE PLACE AND SHOW YOUR TEACHER HOW TO MAKE TAYAMMUM.

LIST THE THREE FARAIDH OF TAYAMMUM IN THE CORRECT ORDER.

1._____

_____

2._____

_____

3._____

_____

Number these Faraidh of Tayammum in the correct order

LESSON FIVE-CONDITIONS FOR TAYAMMUM

When can we perform Tayammum?

1. If there is no water to be found within a one-mile radius then Tayammum can be performed.

2. If a person is very sick and fears that the use of water will cause more illness or harm.

3. If a person is late for a funeral prayer or Eid prayer and he or she fears that they will miss the prayer if they perform Wudhu.

4. If a person fears that they will be attacked by snakes or other animals if they try to fetch water for wudhu.

5. If a person only has enough water for drinking but not enough for wudhu then Tayammum can be performed.

6. All things that break Wudhu also break Tayammum.

EXERCISE FIVE

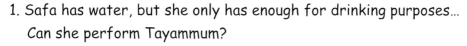

1. Safa has water, but she only has enough for drinking purposes...
   Can she perform Tayammum?

   Yes **No**

   ☐ ☐

2. Hamid cannot find water on his street, but water is available
   within a one-mile radius...

   Can he perform Tayammum?

   Yes **No**

   ☐ ☐

3. Haroon has water available in his area but he fears that a snake
   will attack him...

   Can he perform Tayammum?

   Yes **No**

   ☐ ☐

LESSON SIX-FARAIDH OF SALAH

THERE ARE SEVEN FARAIDH OF SALAH. THIS MEANS THEY ARE COMPULSORY. IF ANY ONE OF THESE ACTS IS MISSED OUT THEN THE SALAH WILL NOT BE ACCEPTED BY ALLAH ⬢ AND WILL HAVE TO BE REPEATED.

Takbeer Tahreema – To say Allahu Akbar for the first time with which Salah begins.

Qiyaam - To stand up straight facing the Qiblah.

Qira'ah - To recite at least three short verses or one long verse of the Holy Qur'aan.

Ruku' - To bend down in such a way that the hands reach the knees.

Sajdah - To place the forehead, nose, hands and knees on the ground bending at least one toe.

Qa'dah Akheera - The last sitting in which Tashahud and Durood Ibrahimi are recited.

Khurooj-Bi-Sunihi - To end the prayer with an action such as Salaam.

EXERCISE SIX

TICK THE FARAIDH OF SALAH FROM THE LIST.

Cleanliness	☐	Qa'dah Akheera	☐
Ruku'	☐	Salaam	☐
Qira'ah	☐	Takbeer Tahreema	☐
Qawmah	☐	Sajdah	☐
Khurooj-Bi-Sunihi	☐	To say Ameen	☐
Thana	☐	Qiyaam	☐

A RAKA'AH IS A SINGLE UNIT OF PRAYER. ONE RAKA'AH CONSISTS OF MAKING TAKBIR AND COMPLETING ALL THE ACTIONS OF PRAYER UNTIL A PERSON COMPLETES THE SECOND PROSTRATION (SAJDAH). SOME HAVE TWO RAKA'AHS, SOME HAVE THREE RAKA'AHS AND OTHERS HAVE FOUR RAKA'AHS. THESE ARE ALSO CALLED CYCLES OF PRAYER.

Fajr

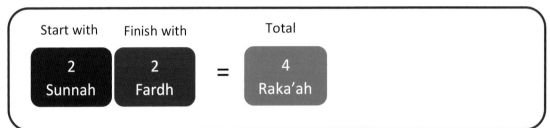

Start with	Finish with		Total
2 Sunnah	2 Fardh	=	4 Raka'ah

Dhuhr

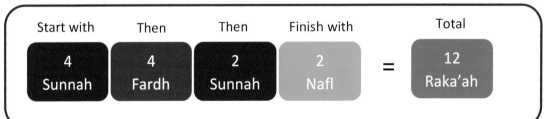

Start with	Then	Then	Finish with		Total
4 Sunnah	4 Fardh	2 Sunnah	2 Nafl	=	12 Raka'ah

Asr

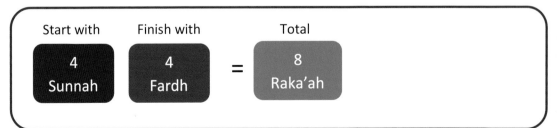

Start with	Finish with		Total
4 Sunnah	4 Fardh	=	8 Raka'ah

Maghrib

Start with	Then	Finish with		Total
3 Fardh	2 Sunnah	2 Nafl	=	7 Raka'ah

Isha

Start with	Then	Then	Then	Then	Finish with
4 Sunnah	4 Fardh	2 Sunnah	2 Nafl	3 Witr	2 Nafl

Total
= 17 Raka'ah

Daily Salah summary chart

Salah	Total Raka'ahs	Sunnah	Fardh	Sunnah	Nafl	Witr	Nafl
Fajr	4	2	2				
Dhuhr	12	4	4	2	2		
Asr	8	4	4				
Maghrib	7		3	2	2		
Isha	17	4	4	2	2	3	2

FILL IN THE GAPS BELOW WITH THE CORRECT NUMBER OF RAKA'AHS.

Fajr

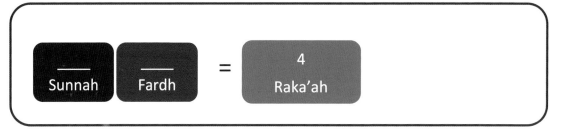

Sunnah ___ | Fardh ___ | = | 4 Raka'ah

Dhuhr

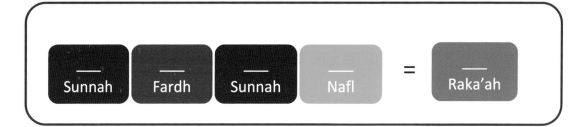

Sunnah ___ | Fardh ___ | Sunnah ___ | Nafl ___ | = | Raka'ah ___

Asr

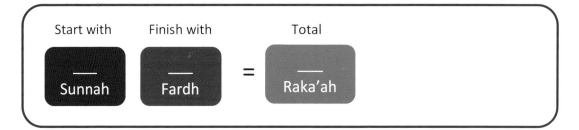

Start with — Sunnah ___ | Finish with — Fardh ___ | = | Total — Raka'ah ___

Maghrib

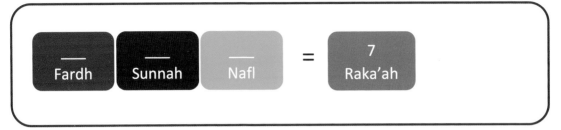

Isha

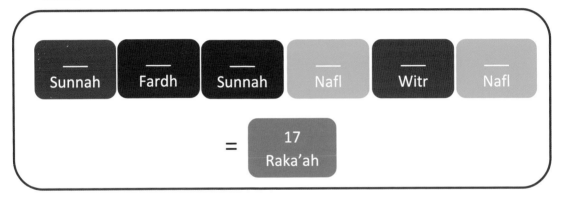

LESSON EIGHT-VIRTUES OF SALAH

PERFORMING THE FIVE DAILY PRAYERS (SALAH) IS AN ESSENTIAL PART OF A MUSLIM'S LIFE. SALAH REMINDS ONE OF THEIR RELATIONSHIP WITH ALLAH ﷻ. IT IS SAID THAT ANY DUAA THAT IS MADE AFTER SALAH IS ACCEPTED.

Allah ﷻ says in the Holy Qur'aan, "Indeed the prayer prevents evil actions and bad deeds."

Our Prophet ﷺ asked his companions, "What do you think if one of you had a river running by his door and he bathed in it five times a day? Would any dirt remain on him? No dirt would remain on him."

He then said, "The example of Salah is similar to this because the five daily prayers would mean that Allah ﷻ would wipe away his sins."

Sayyiduna Rasoolullah ﷺ said, "The first thing a servant of Allah ﷻ will be asked about on the Day of Judgement is the prayer. If it is good, then the rest of his deeds will be good."

The Prophet Muhammad ﷺ said, "Salah in congregation (with Jama'ah) is twenty-seven times greater than Salah performed alone."

1. Which two things will Allah 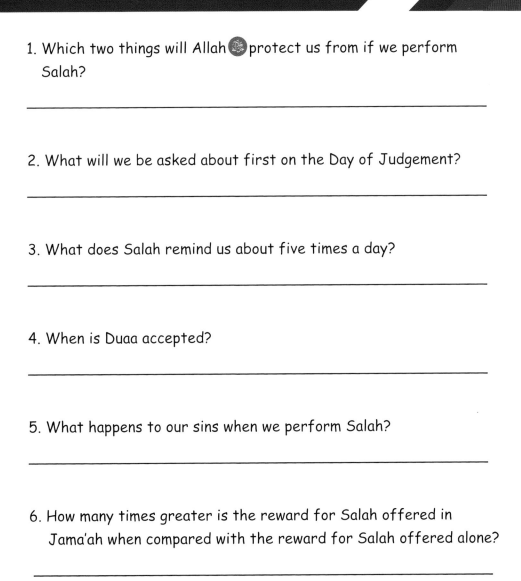 protect us from if we perform Salah?

_____

2. What will we be asked about first on the Day of Judgement?

_____

3. What does Salah remind us about five times a day?

_____

4. When is Duaa accepted?

_____

5. What happens to our sins when we perform Salah?

_____

6. How many times greater is the reward for Salah offered in Jama'ah when compared with the reward for Salah offered alone?

_____

1. Make the Niyyah standing upright and facing the Qiblah.

2. Raise both hands up to the ears saying اَللّٰهُ اَكْبَرْ and the palms should be facing the Qiblah. A woman should raise her hands to her shoulders.

3. Place the palm of your right hand on top of your left hand below the navel. A woman should place her hands on her chest.

4. Whilst praying Salah do not look around. Stand with respect and keep your concentration towards Allah ﷻ.

5. Recite the Thana.

6. Recite Ta'awwudh. اَعُوْذُ بِاللّٰهِ مِنَ الشَّيْطَانِ الرَّجِيمِ

7. Recite Tasmiyah. بِسْمِ اللّٰهِ الرَّحْمٰنِ الرَّحِيمِ

8. Recite Surah Al-Fatiha. Say آمِيْن at the end.

9. Recite any Surah that you have memorised.

10. Say اَللَّهُ اَكْبَرْ and go into Ruku'. Place your hands on the knees and spread the fingers around the knees. Recite سُبْحَانَ رَبِّيَ العَظِيْمِ three times.

A woman should bend just enough to let the fingers reach the knees and keep the head slightly higher than the back. The feet should be joined together at the ankles.

11. Say سَمِعَ اللَّهُ لِمَنْ حَمِدَهُ as you stand up.

12. Whilst you are stood up, say رَبَّنَا وَلَكَ الْحَمْدُ.

13. Say اَللّٰهُ اَكْبَرُ and go into Sajdah by placing the knees on the ground first, followed by the hands then the nose and finally the forehead. The feet should be kept in a vertical position with the toes facing the Qiblah. Ensure that the feet are not lifted from the ground as the Salah will not be valid otherwise. The arms should not touch the sides of the body, nor rest on the ground. The stomach should not touch the thighs.

A female should join her arms with her sides and her stomach with her thighs. She should also join the back of her thighs with her calves and her shins should be placed on the ground. Her feet should point outwards to the right and they should be flat.

14. Whilst in Sajdah recite سُبْحَانَ رَبِّيَ الْأَعْلٰى three times.

15. Say اَللّٰهُ اَكْبَرُ and sit upright. Sit on the left foot with the right foot straight up and the toes facing the Qiblah.

16. Now repeat اَللهُ اَكْبَر and go in to the second Sajdah.

17. After you complete the Sajdah, say اَكْبَرُاللهُ and stand up without putting the hands on the ground. One Raka'ah is now complete.

18. In the second Raka'ah, recite Tasmiyah, Surah Al-Fatiha and another Surah. Perform Ruku', Qawmah and both Sujood. After the second Sajdah do not stand up. Remain in the sitting position and recite Tashahud, Al-Salat Al-Ibrahimi and Duaa Mathoora. A woman should have both of her feet pointing to the right and they should be flat in the Qada position. She should sit on her left buttock. She should keep her hands in the middle of her thighs.

19. Make Salaam by first turning the head towards the right then the left.

Whilst making Salaam, recite السَّلَامُ عَلَيْكُمْ وَرَحْمَةُ اللهِ.

20. Now, make Duaa to Allah .

MODEL PRAYER

Rak'ah 1

Takbeer Tahreema

Qiyaam

Ruku'

Qawmah

- Face Qiblah
- Make Niyyah
- Say اَللهُ اَكْبَرُ raising the hands up to the ears

- Recite Thana
- Recite Ta'awwudh
- Recite Tasmiyah
- Recite Al-Fatiha
- Recite any Surah

- Say اَللهُ اَكْبَرُ whilst going into Ruku'
- Recite 3 times سُبْحَانَ رَبِّيَ الْعَظِيْمِ

- As you stand up recite سَمِعَ اللهُ لِمَنْ حَمِدَه
- Whilst standing recite رَبَّنَا وَ لَكَ الْحَمْدُ

Rak'ah 2

Qiyaam

Ruku'

Qawmah

1st Sujood

- Recite Tasmiyah
- Recite Al-Fatiha
- Recite any Surah

- Say اَللهُ اَكْبَرُ whilst going into Ruku'
- Recite 3 times

- As you stand up recite سَمِعَ اللهُ لِمَنْ حَمِدَه
- Whilst standing recite رَبَّنَا وَ لَكَ الْحَمْدُ

- Say اَللهُ اَكْبَرُ whilst going into Sajdah
- Recite 3 times سُبْحَانَ رَبِّيَ الْأَعْلَى

سُبْحَانَ رَبِّيَ الْعَظِيْمِ

Rak'ah 3

Qiyaam

Ruku'

Qawmah

1st Sujood

- Recite Tasmiyah
- Recite Al-Fatiha

- Say اَللهُ اَكْبَرُ whilst going into Ruku'
- Recite 3 times سُبْحَانَ رَبِّيَ الْعَظِيْمِ

- As you stand up recite سَمِعَ اللهُ لِمَنْ حَمِدَه
- Whilst standing recite رَبَّنَا وَ لَكَ الْحَمْدُ

- Say اَللهُ اَكْبَرُ whilst going into Sajdah
- Recite 3 times سُبْحَانَ رَبِّيَ الْأَعْلَى

Rak'ah 4

Qiyaam

Ruku'

Qawmah

1st Sujood

- Recite Tasmiyah
- Recite Al-Fatiha

- Say اَللهُ اَكْبَرُ whilst going into Ruku'
- Recite 3 times سُبْحَانَ رَبِّيَ الْعَظِيْمِ

- As you stand up recite سَمِعَ اللهُ لِمَنْ حَمِدَه
- Whilst standing recite رَبَّنَا وَ لَكَ الْحَمْدُ

- Say اَللهُ اَكْبَرُ whilst going into Sajdah
- Recite 3 times سُبْحَانَ رَبِّيَ الْأَعْلَى

1st Sujood

- Say اَللّٰهُ اَكْبَرُ whilst going into Sajdah
- Recite 3 times
  سُبْحَانَ رَبِّيَ الْأَعْلَى

Jalsah

- Say اَللّٰهُ اَكْبَرُ and sit up.

2nd Sujood

- Say اَللّٰهُ اَكْبَرُ whilst going into Sajdah
- Recite 3 times
  سُبْحَانَ رَبِّيَ الْأَعْلَى

Jalsah

- Say اَللّٰهُ اَكْبَرُ and sit up.

2nd Sujood

- Say اَللّٰهُ اَكْبَرُ whilst going into Sajdah
- Recite 3 times
  سُبْحَانَ رَبِّيَ الْأَعْلَى

Qa'dah Ula

- Say اَللّٰهُ اَكْبَرُ and sit up.
- Recite Tashahhud
- Stand up saying اَللّٰهُ اَكْبَرُ

Jalsah

- Say اَللّٰهُ اَكْبَرُ and sit up.

2nd Sujood

- Say اَللّٰهُ اَكْبَرُ whilst going into Sajdah
- Recite 3 times
  سُبْحَانَ رَبِّيَ الْأَعْلَى

Note: In Fardh Salah there is no need to pray a Surah in the third and fourth Rak'ah after reciting Surah Al-Fatiha.

Jalsah

Say اَللّٰهُ اَكْبَرُ and sit up.

2nd Sujood

- Say اَللّٰهُ اَكْبَرُ whilst going into Sajdah
- Recite 3 times
  سُبْحَانَ رَبِّيَ الْأَعْلَى

Qa'dah Akheera

- Recite اَللّٰهُ اَكْبَرُ and sit up.
- Recite Tashahhud
- Recite Durood Ibrahimi
- Recite Duaa

Khurooj bi Sunihi

- Finish the Salah by reciting اَلسَّلَامُ عَلَيْكُمْ وَرَحْمَةُ اللّٰهِ turning your head towards the right shoulder then again, the same towards the left shoulder.

Qamar Learning Academy

اَلسِّيرَةُ

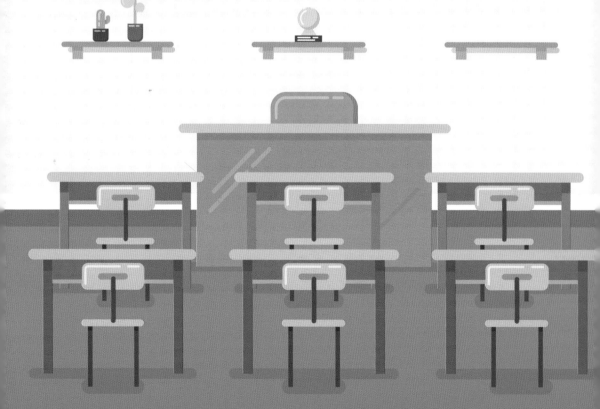

What's in this section?

ARABIA

THE QURAYSH AND THE ARABS

THE HOLY KA'BAH
- Abraha's Plan To Destroy The Ka'bah

THE BIRTH OF OUR PROPHET MUHAMMAD

LIFE IN THE DESERT

CHILDHOOD

JOURNEY TO ASH-SHAAM
- Meeting With Bahira

SECOND TRIP TO ASH-SHAAM

THE MARRIAGE

REBUILDING OF THE HOLY KA'BAH
- Rasoolullah ﷺ Solves The Problem

THE FIRST REVELATION
- Sayyida Khadija ﵂ Comforts Rasoolullah ﷺ

THE ISLAMIC MOVEMENT

TORTURE AND PERSECUTON
- Migration To Abyssinia
- Sayyiduna Jaffar's ﵁ Speech

THE YEAR OF SORROW

MERAJ-UN-NABI
- Meeting With Allah ﷻ

THE FIRST PLEDGE AT AQABA
- The Second Pledge At Aqaba

SEERAH

Arabia is situated in the Middle East. It is an area made up of barren hills, valleys and deserts. The climate is hot and dry. Before the birth of Rasoolullah ﷺ, there were many different groups of people known as tribes. The people who lived in Arabia worshipped idols.

The Arabs were known to drink wine, gamble and kill each other along with many other evil acts. Some of them even used to bury their own daughters alive. The Arabs kept slaves to work, and treated them worse than their animals. There were no laws in Arabia to protect the people.

The Arabs also had many good traits. Quraysh, for example, were known to be very kind and generous towards others. The Arabs were known to be honest people. They were fearless and loved to be free. Most of them were very brave and were very intelligent.

EXERCISE ONE

WRITE THREE FACTS ABOUT ARABIA BELOW.

_____

_____

_____

_____

_____

_____

WRITE THREE BAD THINGS AND THREE GOOD THINGS THE ARABS DID BEFORE ISLAM.

_____

_____

_____

_____

_____

_____

_____

_____

_____

The Arabs were divided into many tribes and clans. No governor or king ruled them all. In Makkah Al-Mukarramah there was a very important tribe called Quraysh. They had the responsibility of looking after the Ka'bah. The Quraysh tribe was made up of many families and the most important family was Banu Hashim. The Prophet Muhammad  was part of this family.

The Quraysh took care of the pilgrims who came to Makkah Al-Mukarramah by providing them with food and water.

The Arabs worshipped many idols. Some of the idols were made up of wood, some from metal and others from stone. They were all different shapes and sizes. Some were shaped like men, some were shaped like women and others took the form of animals.

It is said that there were 360 idols belonging to different tribes in the Holy Ka'bah. Amongst the most famous idols were "Hubal", "Laat" and "Uzza". The people of Makkah Al-Mukarramah believed that these idols had the power to make them rich and successful.

EXERCISE TWO

ANSWER THE QUESTIONS BELOW.

1. Who had the responsibility of looking after the Holy Ka'bah?

   _____

2. What is the name of the family our Prophet Muhammad ﷺ was from?

   _____

3. What were the idols made from?

   _____

4. How many idols were there in the Holy Ka'bah?

   _____

5. What are the names of the three most famous idols?

   _____

Where is the Holy Ka'bah?

The Holy Ka'bah is in Makkah Al-Mukarramah. Its foundation was set by Sayyiduna Adam 👤 and built by Sayyiduna Ibrahim 👤 and his son Ismail 👤.

The Quraysh are the descendants (children) of Sayyiduna Ibrahim 👤. They made their houses around the Ka'bah. As the years passed people began to forget the teachings of Ibrahim 👤 and became idol worshippers.

Sayyiduna Abdul Muttalib 👤 was in charge of the Holy Ka'bah. He was the grandfather of the Holy Prophet 👤 and he never prayed to the idols. He believed in Allah 👤 alone.

In a nearby land called Yemen, there lived a king called Abraha. He was jealous because the Arabs visited Makkah Al-Mukarramah in great numbers. He decided to make a temple in a place called Sanaa. He ordered his people to stop going to Makkah Al-Mukarramah. The people did not listen to him and instead they carried on visiting Makkah Al-Mukarramah.

So Abraha planned to destroy the house of Almighty Allah 👤, the Holy Ka'bah.

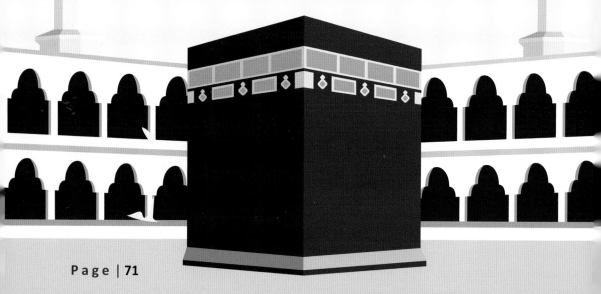

ABRAHA'S PLAN TO DESTROY THE KA'BAH

King Abraha became very angry. He gathered a large army of soldiers and a force of elephants. He set off to go to Makkah Al-Mukarramah to destroy the Holy Ka'bah.

Sayyiduna Abdul Muttalib ؓ heard about the plans and ordered the people to leave the city of Makkah Al-Mukarramah and seek safety in the hills. The people of Makkah Al-Mukarramah watched as Abraha and his army marched towards the Holy Ka'bah. The only hope that Sayyiduna Abdul Muttalib ؓ had was to ask Allah ﷻ for help.

As the elephants were marching towards the Holy Ka'bah they suddenly stopped. They sat down and refused to move.

The sky turned dark and hundreds of birds threw pebbles at the army. They attacked the men of Abraha and most of them died instantly. Abraha also died and his plans had failed.

This is mentioned in Surah Al-Feel.

EXERCISE THREE

DECIDE WHETHER THESE STATEMENTS ARE TRUE OR FALSE BELOW.

	True	False
The Ka'bah is in Makkah Al-Mukarramah.	☐	☐
The Ka'bah was first built by Sayyiduna Ismail ﷺ.	☐	☐
King Abraha was jealous of the Arabs worshipping Allah ﷻ.	☐	☐
Abraha decided to destroy the Ka'bah.	☐	☐
The elephants destroyed the Holy Ka'bah.	☐	☐
Abraha's plans had failed and he was killed.	☐	☐

السِّوَاكُ مَطْهَرَةٌ لِلْفَمِ مَرْضَاةٌ لِلرَّبِّ

"The Miswaak (tooth-stick) purifies the mouth and pleases the Lord"

(Al-Nasai)

The Holy Prophet ﷺ constantly used the Miswaak and commanded to regularly make use of it.

When to make use of a Miswaak:

- Before the recitation of the Qur'aan.
- When the mouth releases a bad smell.
- At the time of performing Wudhu.
- Before and after a meal.
- Before sleeping and upon waking up.
- After entering one's home and before attending a gathering.

Some benefits of using a Miswaak:

- Gaining the pleasure of Allah ﷻ.
- The reward of Salah is multiplied 70 times.
- It improves memory.
- It is a cure for headaches.
- It strengthens the gums and prevents tooth decay.
- It improves eyesight.
- It helps digestion.

Sayyiduna Abdullah ◉, the father of our Prophet Muhammad ◉ was a very handsome and noble man. He was the son of Sayyiduna Abdul Muttalib ◉. A few months after his marriage, he went on a business trip to Al-Shaam. On his way back, he fell ill and passed away in Al-Madina Al-Munawwarah.

Sayyida Aaminah ◉ who was the mother of our Holy Prophet ◉ became worried about how her son would grow up without a father. Sayyida Aaminah ◉ had many great dreams about her son. These dreams gave her peace and comfort. The angels she saw in her dreams told her that her son was going to be a Prophet of Allah ◉

Our Prophet Muhammad ◉ was born on Monday the 12th of Rabi-Ul-Awal in the holy city of Makkah Al-Mukarramah.

Everyone was overjoyed and celebrated the birth of the Holy Prophet ◉. Sayyiduna Abdul Muttalib ◉, who was the grandfather of the Holy Prophet ◉, took him to the Holy Ka'bah when he was only a week old.

To celebrate the birth of Rasoolullah ◉, he prepared a great feast and invited all the leaders of Quraysh, who all attended.

EXERCISE FOUR

ANSWER THE QUESTIONS BELOW.

1. What is the name of Sayyiduna Abdul Muttalib's ﷺ son?

_____

2. On what date was our Prophet Muhammad ﷺ born?

_____

3. Where was our Prophet Muhammad ﷺ born?

_____

4. What did Sayyiduna Abdul Muttalib ﷺ do to celebrate the birth of his grandson?

_____

5. Where was Our Prophet Muhammad ﷺ taken when he was one week old?

_____

Mothers in Makkah Al-Mukarramah would send their children to live in the desert with a wet nurse so that they would grow healthy and strong. Sayyida Aaminah  wanted to send her child, Rasoolullah ﷺ, to the desert but she was poor so she could not afford to pay for an expensive nurse.

The tribe of Banu Saad provided the best nurses. Sayyida Halima was part of this tribe. She came to Makkah Al-Mukarramah with her husband. They were very poor and she was not in good health. She had hardly enough milk for her own child. Their camel and donkey were lean and weak. No rich woman from Quraysh would give her child to Sayyida Halima because she was poor and looked weak.

Sayyida Halima and her husband did not want to leave the city of Makkah Al-Mukarramah without a child they could take care of.

Sayyida Halima came to Sayyida Aaminah and told her that she would like to take care of Rasoolullah ﷺ.

Sayyida Aaminah saw that Halima was a very kind and loving person so she sent Rasoolullah ﷺ to live with them in the desert.

Rasoolullah ﷺ now lived with Sayyida Halima ؓ and her family in the desert.

As soon as our Prophet Muhammad ﷺ entered her house, the health of her animals started to get better. Sayyida Halima ؓ became stronger and wealthier. She and her husband were able to look after our Prophet Muhammad ﷺ very well and they loved him dearly. She knew that all the blessings they received were because of our Prophet Muhammad ﷺ.

When Rasoolullah ﷺ was two years old, he went to visit his mother with Sayyida Halima ؓ. Sayyida Aaminah ؓ was very pleased to see our Prophet Muhammad ﷺ healthy and strong, so she sent him back to the desert again.

The children used to notice strange things happening when they were with our Prophet Muhammad ﷺ. Our Prophet Muhammad ﷺ used to observe other children playing in the fields. They noticed that stones would make Salaam to our Prophet Muhammad ﷺ.

One day, while our Prophet Muhammad ﷺ was in the field with the children. The children saw two people dressed in white come to our Prophet ﷺ. They looked like angels. They laid down our Prophet Muhammad ﷺ and opened his blessed chest. They filled his heart with the Nur (Light) of Allah ﷻ. They then closed his blessed chest and disappeared.

EXERCISE FIVE

WRITE THREE FACTS ABOUT SAYYIDA HALIMA ☙ BELOW.

1._____

_____

2._____

_____

3._____

_____

ANSWER THE QUESTIONS BELOW.

1. What did the angels do when they came to our Prophet Muhammad ﷺ in the fields?

_____

_____

2. What happened to Sayyida Halima ☙ as soon as our Prophet Muhammad ﷺ entered her house?

_____

_____

_____

مَنْ صَلَّى عَلَيَّ وَاحِدَةً صَلَّى اللَّهُ عَلَيْهِ عَشْرًا

"A person who sends one Durood upon me, Allah ﷻ will send down 10 blessings upon him."

(Al-Muslim)

Some of the virtues and benefits of Durood:

- Allah ﷻ will forgive 10 of his sins.
- Allah ﷻ will raise him 10 ranks in the hereafter.
- Allah ﷻ will grant him 10 rewards.
- It will bring the reciter closer to the Prophet Muhammad ﷺ on the Day of Judgement.
- It earns the pleasure of Allah ﷻ.
- It will earn the intercession of Prophet Muhammad ﷺ on the Day of Judgement.
- Reciting Durood before Duaa brings more hope of acceptance.
- It is a reason for forgiveness.
- It will remove one's worries in this world and the hereafter.

LESSON SIX-CHILDHOOD

When Rasoolullah ﷺ was almost six years old, after having spent many years with Sayyida Halima ﵃ in the desert, she decided to take him back to Makkah Al-Mukarramah and return him to Sayyida Aaminah ﵂ .

Sayyida Aaminah ﵂ decided to take him to Al-Madinah Al-Munawwarah to see his relatives and show him his beloved father's grave. The two went with their servant, Umm Ayman.

After visiting the places in Al-Madina Al-Munawwarah, they set off to return home. On their way home, Sayyida Aaminah ﵂ fell very ill. She did not recover from her illness and passed away at a place called Al-Abwa. Rasoolullah ﷺ was alone at the age of six. Umm Ayman took our Prophet Muhammad ﷺ home to his grandfather, Sayyiduna Abdul Muttalib ﵁ .

Sayyiduna Abdul Muttalib ﵁ was now taking care of our Prophet Muhammad ﷺ. He loved his grandson and cared for him greatly. When Rasoolullah ﷺ was eight, his grandfather passed away at the age of 82. Rasoolullah ﷺ was now even more alone and very sad.

Sayyiduna Rasoolullah's ﷺ uncle, Abu Talib took our Prophet Muhammad ﷺ to his home to look after him. Our Prophet Muhammad ﷺ grew up under the care of Abu Talib whom he loved and stayed close to all the time.

EXERCISE SIX

ANSWER THE QUESTIONS BELOW.

1. At what age did our Prophet Muhammad ﷺ return to Makkah Al-Mukarramah?

   _____

2. Why did our Prophet Muhammad ﷺ visit Al-Madina Al-Munawwarah?

   _____

3. Where did Sayyida Aaminah ﴿﴾ pass away and who took our Prophet Muhammad ﷺ back to Makkah Al-Mukarramah?

   _____

4. When Rasoolullah ﷺ was 8 years old, which sad event took place?

   _____

Abu Talib was a merchant but he was not very successful and he was not very wealthy. Our Prophet Muhammad ﷺ tried his best to help his uncle in whatever way he could.

When Rasoolullah ﷺ was 12 years old, Abu Talib decided to go on a business trip to Al-Shaam (Syria).

Abu Talib went with his goods on camels and donkeys as they were used as a means of transport.

Abu Talib told Sayyiduna Muhammad ﷺ that it would be better if he stayed at home as the roads were dangerous. Rasoolullah ﷺ pleaded with his uncle to take him and he eventually agreed.

This was Rasoolullah's ﷺ first trip to Al-Shaam. The two travelled together until they reached the city of Busra, which was in the south of Al-Shaam.

MEETING WITH BAHIRA

A Christian monk called Bahira was observing the caravan that came into the city of Busra. He approached the men and invited them to his house. He made preparations to host them with a meal.

While they were eating, Bahira kept staring at Rasoolullah ﷺ. He saw that Sayyiduna Muhammad ﷺ was a very noble young man, who was generous and humble. He spoke to Rasoolullah ﷺ and he recognised the signs that this young man was the last Prophet of Allah ﷻ.

He asked Rasoolullah ﷺ to lift up his blessed shirt. When Rasoolullah ﷺ lifted up his shirt, Bahira saw the seal of Prophethood on his blessed back. He was amazed and kissed the seal.

The Christian monk advised Abu Talib to return to Makkah Al-Mukarramah and give full protection to Rasoolullah ﷺ as people would attempt to kill him if they found out who he ﷺ was.

After trading in Busra and making a good profit, Abu Talib and Sayyiduna Muhammad ﷺ returned to Makkah Al-Mukarramah.

EXERCISE SEVEN

DESCRIBE THE FIRST TRIP TO AL-SHAAM IN YOUR OWN WORDS BELOW. SHARE IT WITH YOUR TEACHER BY READING IT OUT ALOUD.

_____

_____

_____

_____

_____

_____

_____

_____

_____

_____

_____

_____

_____

_____

_____

_____

_____

_____

_____

_____

_____

مَنْ كَانَ يُؤْمِنُ بِاللَّهِ وَالْيَوْمِ الْآخِرِ فَلْيَقُلْ خَيْرًا أَوْ لِيَصْمُتْ

"Whoever has faith in Allah ﷻ and the Last Day should either speak what is good or remain silent."

(Al-Bukhari/Muslim)

Speaking checklist:

- Speak clearly.
- Speak from in front of a person and not from behind him.
- Never engage in gossip, slander or backbiting.
- Stay away from any talk which does not benefit one in religious or worldly affairs.
- Youngsters should not call their elders by their names. They should adopt a name or title of respect and honour.
- If a person mistakes you for someone else, immediately correct them.
- Do not interrupt people when they are having a conversation. Speak only when asked to do so.
- When someone speaks unfriendly of your elders, do not inform them as doing so will cause grief for them.

LESSON EIGHT-SECOND TRIP TO AL-SHAAM

Rasoolullah ﷺ was now a young man. He received a business offer from a wealthy widow called Sayyida Khadija Bint Khuwaylid رضي الله عنها. She wanted him to look after her business and sell goods for her. She heard that our Prophet Muhammad ﷺ was a very honest man so she hoped to employ him. She promised to give Rasoolullah ﷺ a share in the profits. Rasoolullah ﷺ accepted the offer.

Rasoolullah ﷺ set out for Al-Shaam for a second time as he wanted to help Sayyida Khadija رضي الله عنها sell her goods. The servant of Sayyida Khadija رضي الله عنها, Maysara, accompanied our Prophet Muhammad ﷺ.

Rasoolullah's ﷺ trip to Al-Shaam was very successful. He sold all the goods that he had taken on the caravan. He then bought what was required and made his way back to Makkah Al-Mukarramah.

He made huge profits for her through his intelligence, skill and honesty. Sayyida Khadija رضي الله عنها did not expect to make so much profit and was very pleased.

EXERCISE EIGHT

ANSWER THE QUESTIONS BELOW.

1. Who did Rasoolullah  receive an offer from?

_____

2. Why did Sayyida Khadija want to employ our Prophet Muhammad?

_____

3. Who accompanied Rasoolullah on the trip to Al-Shaam?

_____

4. Why was Rasoolullah successful in the business he did?

_____

5. How was Sayyida Khadija feeling about the business he did?

_____

Sayyida Khadija ﷺ was a well-respected woman amongst the people of Makkah Al-Mukarramah. She was from a noble family and was also respected as a good merchant. People referred to her as Al-Taahira, the 'pure one'.

Maysara told Sayyida Khadija ﷺ that Sayyiduna Muhammad ﷺ had been very successful in his business dealings in Al-Shaam. Sayyida Khadija ﷺ was pleased and she sent Maysara to Rasoolullah ﷺ with a marriage proposal. Rasoolullah ﷺ accepted the proposal. He was 25 years old at the time and Sayyida Khadija ﷺ was 40 years old.

Sayyiduna Rasoolullah ﷺ adopted a slave from Sayyida Khadija ﷺ called Sayyiduna Zaid ﷺ and she gave him much of her wealth.

Sayyiduna Rasoolullah ﷺ was now a wealthy man who supported many poor people. He helped the orphans, paid off debts and freed many slaves.

Rasoolullah ﷺ and Sayyida Khadija ﷺ had six children. They had two sons and four daughters.

Rasoolullah's ﷺ sons were Sayyiduna Qasim ﷺ and Sayyiduna Abdullah ﷺ.

Rasoolullah's ﷺ daughters were Sayyida Zainab ﷺ, Sayyida Ruqayyah ﷺ, Sayyida Umm Kulthum ﷺ and Sayyida Fatima ﷺ.

Rasoolullah ﷺ and Sayyida Khadija ﷺ loved each other deeply and they had a special friendship. Sayyida Khadija ﷺ would sacrifice all she had for Rasoolullah ﷺ.

EXERCISE NINE

FILL IN THE GAPS BELOW.

1. Sayyida Khadija 🕌 sent_____ to Rasoolullah 🕌 with a marriage proposal.

2. When Rasoolullah 🕌 was ____ years old he married Sayyida Khadija 🕌 who was____ years old.

3. Sayyida Khadija 🕌 gave much of her wealth to Rasoolullah 🕌 and gave him a slave called _____.

4. Rasoolullah 🕌 and Sayyida Khadija 🕌 had____ children.

5. Rasoolullah's 🕌 sons' names were:

_____

_____

6. Rasoolullah's 🕌 daughters' names were:

_____

_____

_____

_____

When Rasoolullah ﷺ was 35 years old, the leaders of Quraysh decided to rebuild the Holy Ka'bah. The Holy Ka'bah needed repairs after a sudden flood had damaged and cracked the walls.

The rebuilding of the Holy Ka'bah began. Rasoolullah ﷺ took part in rebuilding and helped the Quraysh in building the walls. The walls of the Holy Ka'bah were raised much higher than they had been before.

It was time to place the black stone, known as Al-Hajr-ul-Aswad, in its place on the East side of the Holy Ka'bah. The placing of Al-Hajr-ul-Aswad was seen as an honour by all the people of Makkah Al-Mukarramah. Especially by the Quraysh as it was sacred to them.

During this time, arguments broke out between different tribes. They were arguing about who should place the black stone in its place. This argument almost led to a war between the tribes in Makkah Al-Mukarramah. Someone needed to resolve the dispute.

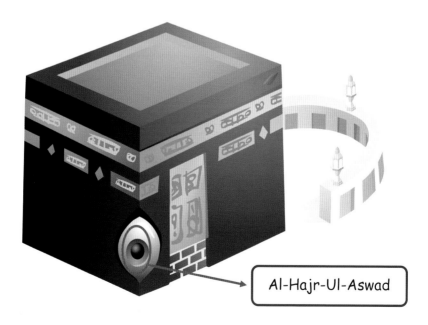

Al-Hajr-Ul-Aswad

RASOOLULLAH ﷺ SOLVES THE PROBLEM

An old man who was named Shaiba, suggested an idea. He said, "Let the first man to enter through the gate of Al-Haram tomorrow morning decide the matter in dispute amongst us."

The leaders agreed and returned home. The next morning, they all waited to see who would enter through the gate of Al-Haram first. The first man to enter was Rasoolullah ﷺ.

The people of Makkah Al-Mukarramah began to shout it is "Al-Ameen." They knew he was a fair judge and would bring peace.

Sayyiduna Muhammad ﷺ said, "Give me a cloak."

When the cloak was brought to him, he spread it out on the ground and placed the black stone on it. He commanded one leader from each tribe to come and hold a corner of the cloak. He told them to raise the cloak. Rasoolullah ﷺ then lifted the stone with his blessed hands and placed it on the corner of the Holy Ka'bah.

The people of Makkah Al-Mukarramah were very pleased and they felt honoured. All their disputes had been settled and Rasoolullah ﷺ had prevented a war between the tribes of the holy city.

DESCRIBE THE EVENTS OF THE REBUILDING OF THE HOLY KA'BAH AFTER IT WAS DAMAGED.

_____

_____

_____

_____

_____

_____

_____

_____

_____

_____

_____

_____

_____

_____

اَلدُّعَاءُ هُوَ الْعِبَادَةُ

"Supplication (Duaa) is worship."

(Abu Dawud / Al-Tirmidhi)

In another narration, Our Prophet Muhammadﷺ mentioned, "Any Muslim who raises his hands towards Allah ﷻ to ask for anything, Allah ﷻ surely grants him that particular thing he wishes. Either he is granted that thing immediately, or it is reserved for him in the future or in the hereafter."

Lessons learnt from this Hadith:

- If the desired thing is beneficial, it is given immediately.
- If the desired thing brings no immediate benefit, then it is delayed for an appropriate time.
- The one who makes Duaa is given that which is better than what they asked for, either in this world or the hereafter.
- A Duaa must be made with humbleness and sincerity and can be made in any language.
- For a Duaa to be accepted, one should make sure their food and earnings are Halaal.

In no way does any Duaa go unheard by Allah ﷻ .

LESSON ELEVEN-FIRST REVELATION

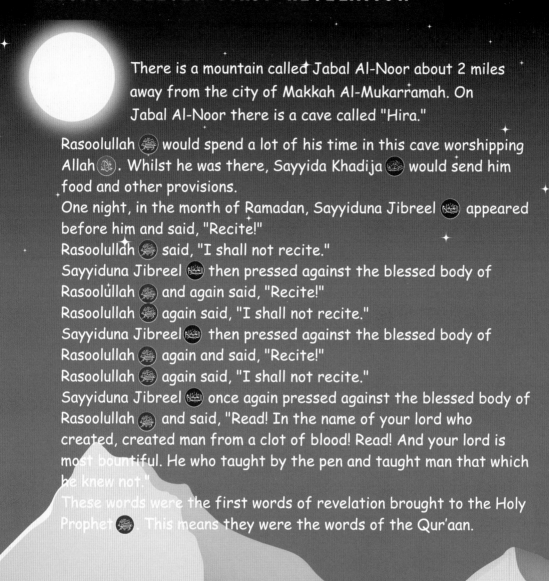

There is a mountain called Jabal Al-Noor about 2 miles away from the city of Makkah Al-Mukarramah. On Jabal Al-Noor there is a cave called "Hira."

Rasoolullah ﷺ would spend a lot of his time in this cave worshipping Allah ﷻ. Whilst he was there, Sayyida Khadija رضي الله عنها would send him food and other provisions.

One night, in the month of Ramadan, Sayyiduna Jibreel عليه السلام appeared before him and said, "Recite!"

Rasoolullah ﷺ said, "I shall not recite."

Sayyiduna Jibreel عليه السلام then pressed against the blessed body of Rasoolullah ﷺ and again said, "Recite!"

Rasoolullah ﷺ again said, "I shall not recite."

Sayyiduna Jibreel عليه السلام then pressed against the blessed body of Rasoolullah ﷺ again and said, "Recite!"

Rasoolullah ﷺ again said, "I shall not recite."

Sayyiduna Jibreel عليه السلام once again pressed against the blessed body of Rasoolullah ﷺ and said, "Read! In the name of your lord who created, created man from a clot of blood! Read! And your lord is most bountiful. He who taught by the pen and taught man that which he knew not."

These words were the first words of revelation brought to the Holy Prophet ﷺ. This means they were the words of the Qur'aan.

SAYYIDA KHADIJA  COMFORTS RASOOLULLAH

Rasoolullah 🕌 went home and he was worried. He told his wife Sayyida Khadija 🕌 all that had happened to him in the Cave of Hiraa. Sayyida Khadija 🕌 comforted him and she told him, "O Muhammad 🕌, you are a good person. You are kind to the poor. You love the orphans and comfort the widows. You always speak the truth. Allah 🕌 loves such people. Surely, Allah 🕌 will protect you. He will never let any harm come to you."

Rasoolullah 🕌 and Sayyida Khadija 🕌 went to her cousin, Waraqa bin Naufal, for advice on the matter. They explained to him what had happened and he assured them that Rasoolullah 🕌 was the messenger of Allah 🕌. He also told them that the Angel Jibreel 🕌 had also appeared to other prophets of Allah 🕌.

EXERCISE ELEVEN

IN YOUR OWN WORDS, DESCRIBE WHAT HAPPENED WHEN RASOOLULLAH ﷺ MET JIBREEL عليه السلام FOR THE FIRST TIME.

_____

_____

_____

_____

_____

_____

_____

_____

IN YOUR OWN WORDS, DESCRIBE THE EVENT WHEN RASOOLULLAH ﷺ WENT TO SEE WARAQA BIN NAUFAL.

_____

_____

_____

_____

_____

_____

_____

_____

_____

_____

_____

_____

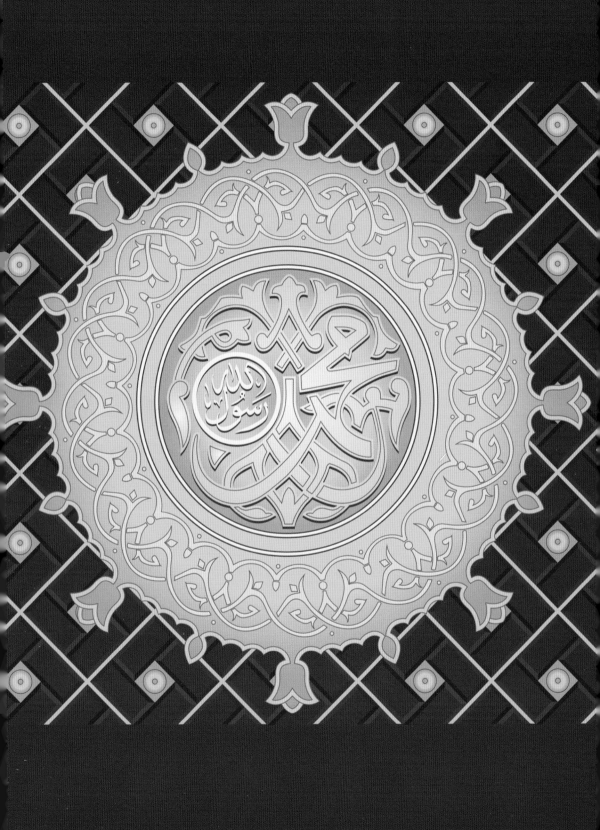

LESSON TWELVE-THE ISLAMIC MOVEMENT

The revelation that was received by Sayyiduna Rasoolullah ﷺ marked the beginning of the Islamic Movement. The aim of the movement, with Rasoolullah ﷺ as its leader, was to invite the people to Islam and establish the laws of Allah ﷻ on earth. Soon thereafter, Sayyiduna Rasoolullah ﷺ invited his close friends and relatives to Islam.

Sayyiduna Ali ؓ was the son of Abu Talib and the cousin of our Prophet Muhammad ﷺ. He was a young boy and he spent much of his time in the house and company of Rasoolullah ﷺ and his family. He would listen to Sayyiduna Rasoolullah ﷺ and Sayyida Khadija ؓ reciting the Holy Qur'aan.

One day, Rasoolullah ﷺ invited him to accept Islam. He did not accept Islam immediately for he felt the need to consult his father, Abu Talib, about it first. The next morning however, he rushed to Rasoolullah ﷺ and accepted Islam whilst he was just 10 years old.

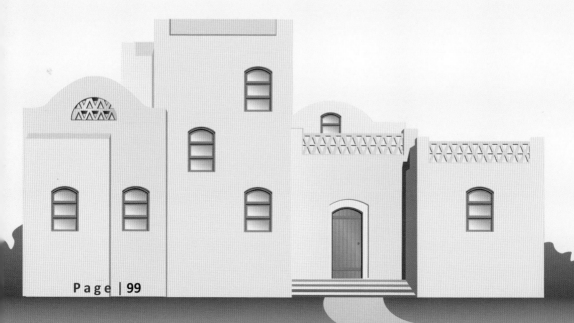

ANSWER THE QUESTIONS BELOW.

1. What is the aim of the Islamic movement?

_____

2. What is the name of Sayyiduna Ali's ﷺ father?

_____

3. Why did Sayyiduna Ali ﷺ not accept Islam straight away?

_____

4. How old was Sayyiduna Ali ﷺ when he accepted Islam?

_____

Many of the Quraysh did not like the message of Islam. They were worried because their idols were not being worshipped. The Quraysh tried to bribe Rasoolullah ﷺ in exchange for gifts or anything else that he wanted. But they failed to persuade him to agree to anything that would be harmful to Islam.

The Quraysh were very upset and started to torture and persecute Muslims.

Sayyiduna Bilal رضي الله عنه was a companion of Rasoolullah ﷺ. The Quraysh laid him flat on his back upon hot sand and placed a heavy stone on his chest. Sayyiduna Bilal رضي الله عنه was even beaten whilst his hands were tied behind his back.

Another companion, Sayyiduna Uthman رضي الله عنه, was a rich and prosperous man. He was also tied with rope and beaten by his own uncle.

Sayyiduna Abu Dharr رضي الله عنه, recited the Qur'aan in a loud voice near the Ka'bah. Some of the Quraysh who were present immediately set upon him and beat him unconscious.

Life in Makkah Al-Mukarramah had become very difficult for the Muslims.

MIGRATION TO ABYSSINIA

Life in Makkah Al-Mukarramah became unbearable for the Muslims. Sayyiduna Rasoolullah ﷺ was concerned for their safety and advised the Muslims to migrate (make Hijrah) to the land of Abyssinia (Ethiopia) in Africa.

"Hijrah" means to migrate from one's own country usually when one does not have freedom of religion there. This happened after the 5th year of prophethood.

The first group of Muslims that left for Abyssinia by ship included 11 men and 4 women.

The King of Abyssinia, Najashi (Negus), was a very noble and fair person. He was a Christian who did not object to the Muslims living in his country. The Muslims were able to live peacefully and practise Islam. When the persecution of the Muslims in Makkah Al-Mukarramah became more serious, many more Muslims left Makkah Al-Mukarramah and settled in Abyssinia.

When the Kuffar of Quraysh heard about the migration of Muslims to Abyssinia, they became angry. They went to the court of Negus. They told Negus that the Muslims were following a new religion and that they should be removed from Abyssinia. Negus was a very fair man. He asked the Muslims to explain the whole situation to him.

Sayyiduna Jafar 🟤, the son of Abu Talib, addressed Negus and all those present.

He said, "O King! We were in a very bad state. We were worshipping idols and treating everyone badly."

"Then Allah 🟤 sent us a Prophet 🟤. He told us to worship Allah 🟤 alone and to give up the idols, the stones, which we used to worship.

"He commanded us to hold prayers. We believed in him and what he brought to us from Allah 🟤 and we followed him in what he had asked us to do."

"After this, the people attacked us and told us to return to the worship of idols. They made life difficult for us in Makkah Al-Mukarramah and we came to your country so that we could live in peace."

Sayyiduna Jafar 🟤 then read Surah Maryam, which is a chapter of the Qur'aan. It was about the Prophet Isa 🟤. Negus understood the words of the Qur'aan. Its message about Sayyiduna Isa 🟤 and Sayyida Maryam 🟤 made him cry while listening to it.

Negus sent the Kuffar of Quraysh back to Makkah Al-Mukarramah and he told the Muslims that he would protect them so that they could live in his country in peace. The Muslims were overjoyed as the Kuffar had failed in their plans to harm the Muslims.

EXERCISE THIRTEEN

ANSWER THE QUESTIONS BELOW.

1. What is the meaning of Hijrah?

_____

_____

_____

2. How many people were in the first group that migrated to Abyssinia?

_____

3. What did the Kuffar do when they heard about the migration?

_____

_____

4. What did Sayyiduna Jafar ﷺ say to Negus?

_____

_____

_____

_____

_____

LESSON FOURTEEN-YEAR OF SORROW

Sayyiduna Rasoolullah ﷺ was now 50 years old and it had been 10 years since he had received the first Revelation of the Qur'aan from Almighty Allah ﷻ. More sorrow and grief was to face him that year.

This year is called "The Year of Sorrow" or "Aam-al-Huzn." Abu Talib passed away at the age of 82. Abu Talib's death was a great loss to our Prophet Muhammad ﷺ because Abu Talib always protected him from the Kuffar. Abu Talib managed to convince Banu Hashim and Banu Muttalib to protect our Prophet Muhammad ﷺ. Now that he was gone, Sayyiduna Rasoolullah ﷺ did not have strong support against the enemies.

Sayyiduna Rasoolullah's ﷺ beloved wife, Sayyida Khadija ﵁, also passed away on the 10th of Ramadaan at the age of 65. Her demise was a great loss to Sayyiduna Rasoolullah ﷺ. She had always supported him in his mission. She comforted him through all the hardships that he had faced. She had helped him financially and gave away all her wealth in the service of Islam. Sayyiduna Rasoolullah ﷺ had loved her very much and he used to remember her very often after she had passed away.

EXERCISE FOURTEEN

1. How old was Rasoolullah ﷺ when Sayyida Khadija ؓ and his uncle, Abu Talib, passed away?

_____

2. What is the "Year of Sorrow" called in Arabic?

_____

3. Write two reasons why Abu Talib was a great loss to Rasoolullah ﷺ.

_____

_____

_____

_____

4. How old was Sayyida Khadija ؓ when she passed away and what date was it?

_____

LESSON FIFTEEN-MERAJ UN NABI ﷺ

The Prophet Muhammad ﷺ was sleeping in the house of Umm Haani ﵂. One night when Sayyiduna Jibreel ﵇ came to him, he gave him the good news that Allah ﷻ wished him to be in His Presence. Sayyiduna Jibreel ﵇ took him to the Holy Ka'bah. He then opened the blessed chest of Sayyiduna Rasoolullah ﷺ, washed it with Zam Zam water and filled it with the Nur (Light) of Allah ﷻ. They then mounted the "Buraq," a blessed beast from Jannah that was ridden as a mode of transport. Buraq's every stride took them as far as the eye could see. They set off and travelled to the holy city of Jerusalem.

They stopped in Jerusalem at the Al-Aqsa mosque. There, Sayyiduna Rasoolullah ﷺ met all the Prophets of the past and led them in Salah.

From Jerusalem, Sayyiduna Rasoolullah ﷺ was taken to the Heavens. The heavens have many levels and Rasoolullah ﷺ met many people as well as seeing some amazing things there.

- In the 1st Heaven - He was met by Sayyiduna Adam ﵇
- 2nd Heaven - He was met by Sayyiduna Yahya ﵇ and Sayyiduna Isa ﵇
- 3rd Heaven – He was met by Sayyiduna Yusuf ﵇
- 4th Heaven – He was met by Sayyiduna Idris ﵇
- 5th Heaven – He was met by Sayyiduna Haroon ﵇
- 6th Heaven – He was met by Sayyiduna Musa ﵇
- 7th Heaven – He was met by Sayyiduna Ibrahim ﵇

Sayyiduna Rasoolullah ﷺ saw the beauty of the Gardens of Jannah, which Allah ﷻ has promised to those who obey him. He also saw the terrible sights of Jahannam, where evil people will go after death.

MEETING WITH ALLAH

Finally, Sayyiduna Jibreel brought him to a tree called "Sidrah-Al-Muntaha." It was a place where no Angel or human being could go beyond and no one else would ever go thereafter. He had to travel on his own until he was in the presence of Allah. He saw Allah with his own blessed eyes.

Allah spoke directly to His Beloved Prophet Sayyiduna Rasoolullah. He was given the following by Allah:

- Five daily prayers which became compulsory for all Muslims.

- The last portion of Surah Al-Baqarah.

- He was promised that Muslims who believed in Allah would be granted Jannah.

- He was promised that Allah would reward those Muslims who performed good deeds.

Sayyiduna Rasoolullah then returned to the home of Umm Haani.

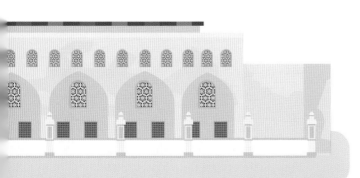

EXERCISE FIFTEEN

ANSWER THE QUESTIONS BELOW.

1. Describe the incident of the splitting of the blessed chest of Rasoolullah ﷺ.

   _____

   _____

   _____

2. What transport was used to travel to Jerusalem?

   _____

3. Name the Prophets Rasoolullah ﷺ met in each heaven.

   _____

   _____

   _____

   _____

   _____

   _____

   _____

4. Which tree was Rasoolullah ﷺ brought to?

_____

5. Who did Rasoolullah ﷺ see on this journey?

_____

6. List the four things that were granted to Rasoolullah ﷺ by Allah ﷻ.

_____

_____

_____

_____

_____

LESSON SIXTEEN-FIRST PLEDGE OF AQABA

Aqaba is a place between the cave of Hira and Mina near Makkah Al-Mukarramah.

In the 11th year of Rasoolullah's ﷺ mission, 6 men from Al-Madinah Al-Munawwarah met him at Aqaba. He told them about Islam and they pledged their allegiance to Rasoolullah ﷺ. They then returned to their homes and spread the message of Islam in their city, Al-Madinah Al-Munawwarah.

The following year, 12 men from the tribe of Khazraj in Al-Madinah Al-Munawwarah came to Sayyiduna Rasoolullah ﷺ and accepted Islam. They made the following pledge with him.

- Not to make partners with Allah ﷻ.
- Not to steal.
- Not to kill their daughters.
- Not to bring false charges against an innocent person.
- To obey Sayyiduna Rasoolullah ﷺ.

This was the first pledge of Al-Aqaba.

Sayyiduna Rasoolullah ﷺ promised those that kept the pledge that they would be granted Jannah as a reward. He also sent Sayyiduna Musab bin Umair رضي الله عنه to Al-Madinah Al-Munawwarah to teach people about the religion of Islam.

SECOND PLEDGE AT AQABA

In the 13th year of the mission, 73 men and 2 women met Rasoolullah ﷺ at Aqaba. They urged him to come to their city. Sayyiduna Abbas رضي الله عنه, who as was not yet a Muslim, asked the people of Al-Madinah Al-Munawwarah to promise that they would protect Rasoolullah ﷺ at all times. The people promised to do so. At the same time, they were anxious to hear what Sayyiduna Rasoolullah ﷺ had to say.

Sayyiduna Rasoolullah ﷺ recited verses from the Qur'aan. He then explained the principles of Islam (to them). Thereafter, he said, "I accept your allegiance on the condition that you would protect me in the same way as you would protect your women and children."

They agreed to support him. Sayyiduna Rasoolullah ﷺ was satisfied with their response.

"What shall be for us, O Prophet of Allah ﷻ, if we remain firm in our pledge?" they asked.

"Paradise," was the reply.

They all stretched out their hands, placing them together, and took the pledge. "We pledge that we will hear and obey in times of distress and in times of comfort, and whatever befalls us of happiness and anguish, and that we will speak the truth wherever we be, not fearing disapproval of the oppressors, in the path of Allah ﷻ."

This was the second pledge at Al-Aqaba.

ANSWER THE QUESTIONS ABOUT THE FIRST PLEDGE BELOW.

1. Where is Aqaba situated?

_____

2. What five pledges were made by the people to Rasoolullah ﷺ at the first pledge?

_____

_____

_____

_____

_____

_____

3. What did Rasoolullah ﷺ promise them?

_____

_____

1. How many people met Rasoolullah ﷺ in the 13ᵗʰ year of the mission?

_____

2. What did Sayyiduna Abbas ؓ tell the people of Al-Madinah Al-Munawwarah?

_____

_____

3. How did Rasoolullah ﷺ respond to their pledge of allegiance?

_____

_____

_____

4. What was the reply of Rasoolullah ﷺ when they asked what they would receive?

_____

_____

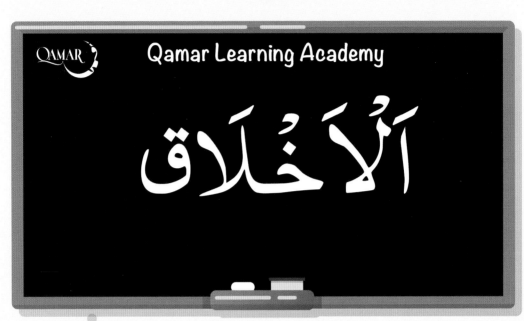

Qamar Learning Academy

اَلْاَخْلَاق

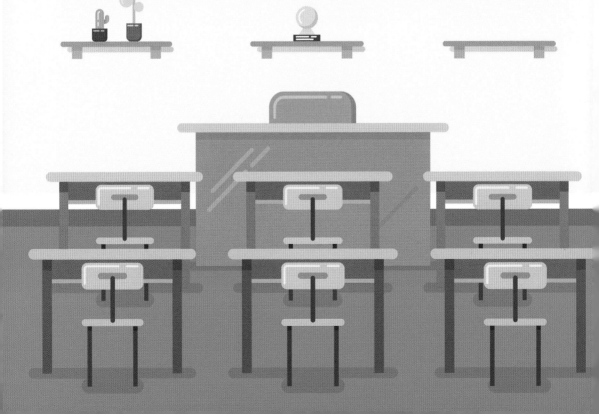

What's in this section?

RECITING THE QUR'AAN

- Virtues Of Reciting The Qur'aan
- Teachings Of The Qur'aan

THE MASJID

- The Prophet's  Sayings

PROPHETIC CHARACTER

MANNERS OF EATING AND DRINKING

WALKING

TALKING TO OTHERS

- The Date Palm Tree

VALUING YOUR TIME

- Our Prophet Muhammad's Guidance

GIVING GIFTS

- Imaam Abu Hanifa and The Gift

HONOURING OUR NEIGHBOURS

- Malik Bin Dinar And His Neighbours

AKHLAQ

اخلاق و کردار

THE QUR'AAN IS THE BOOK OF ALLAH ﷻ WHICH WAS REVEALED TO OUR PROPHET MUHAMMAD ﷺ THROUGH ANGEL JIBREEL ﷺ TO SHOW PEOPLE THE RIGHT PATH. THE QUR'AAN IS THE KEY BOOK FOR MUSLIMS. THE PROPHET ﷺ STATED, "THE BEST AMONG YOU IS THE ONE WHO LEARNS THE QUR'AAN AND TEACHES IT (TO OTHERS)."

Reciting the Qur'aan checklist

I Will:

- ☑ Make Wudhu so that I am in a clean state.

- ☑ Sit in a respectful place in a respectful manner.

- ☑ Place the Qur'aan on a bench when reciting.

- ☑ Recite the Qur'aan with the correct Tajweed rules.

- ☑ Recite Ta'awwudh and Tasmiyah before I begin to recite.

- ☑ Recite slowly.

- ☑ Not talk when reciting the Qur'aan.

- ☑ Rest the Qur'aan on a high place.

- ☑ Treat the Qur'aan with respect.

- ☑ Try to learn the meaning of the Qur'aan.

VIRTUES OF RECITING THE QUR'AAN

The Qur'aan will be a proof for you on the Day of Judgement.

You will be from the best of people.

Your status in this life will be raised.

Reading the Qur'aan is fulfilling a duty of Islam.

There are 10 rewards for every letter you recite from the Qur'aan.

The one who memorises the Qur'aan will enter Jannah.

Your position in paradise is decided by your understanding of the Qur'aan.

Whoever teaches his child the Qur'aan will wear a crown in Jannah.

The reciters of the Qur'aan will be in the company of the best angels

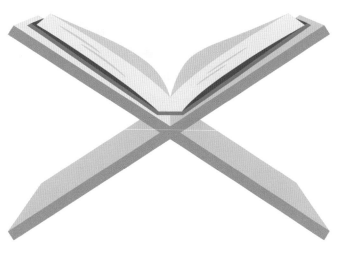

WRITE 6 TEACHINGS OF THE QUR'AAN BELOW.

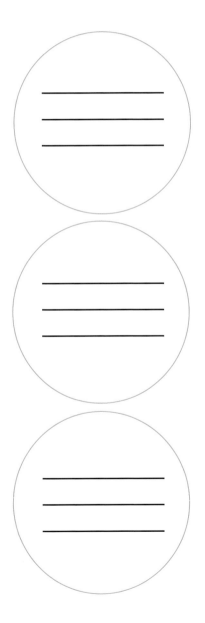

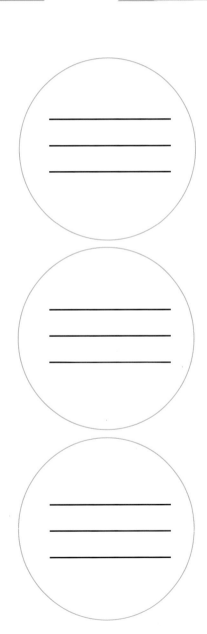

LESSON TWO-THE MASJID

THE MASJID IS THE HOUSE OF ALLAH . THIS IS THE PLACE WHERE MUSLIMS GO TO PRAY 5 TIMES A DAY. IT IS THE PLACE FROM WHICH THE MESSAGE OF KNOWLEDGE AND PEACE IS SPREAD. WE MUST RESPECT THE MASJID. WE MUST LOVE IT. THE PROPHET SAID, "THE ONE WHO LOVES THE HOUSE OF ALLAH, ALLAH LOVES HIM." HE ALSO SAID, "THE ONE WHO GOES TO THE MASJID, ALLAH WILL PREPARE A PLACE FOR HIM IN JANNAH EVERY TIME HE VISITS."

I will:

- ✅ Wear clean clothes to the Masjid.
- ✅ Clean my mouth and remove any bad smell.
- ✅ Place my shoes on the shoe rack.
- ✅ Enter the Masjid with the right foot and recite the Duaa.
- ✅ Reply to the Adhaan.
- ✅ Make dua or Dhikr before Jama'ah.
- ✅ Not disturb others.
- ✅ Not talk, laugh, joke or shout at anyone.
- ✅ Keep the Masjid clean.
- ✅ Respect the people who attend the Masjid, especially the Imaam.
- ✅ Not walk in front of anyone who is performing Salah.
- ✅ Attend speeches to learn.
- ✅ Help the Masjid by donating money in charity.
- ✅ Leave the Masjid with my left foot and recite the Duaa.

The one who loves the house of Allah ﷻ, Allah ﷻ loves him.
(Tabarani)

Allah ﷻ will ask on the Day of Judgement, "Where are my neighbours?" The Angels will say, "Who could possibly be your neighbour?" Allah ﷻ will reply, "The one who frequented the mosque."
(Hilya Al-Awliyaa)

The one who performed Wudhu correctly in his own house and then made way to the Masjid, he is the guest of Allah ﷻ.
(Tabarani)

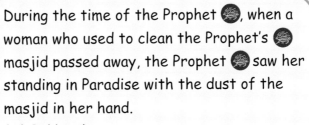

During the time of the Prophet ﷺ, when a woman who used to clean the Prophet's ﷺ masjid passed away, the Prophet ﷺ saw her standing in Paradise with the dust of the masjid in her hand.
(Al-Bukhari)

EXERCISE TWO

WRITE 5 THINGS WE SHOULD DO IN A MASJID.

1. _____

2. _____

3. _____

4. _____

5. _____

A companion went to see our mother Sayyida Ayesha 🕮 and asked about the character of the Messenger of Allah 🕮. She asked him, "Do you not read the Qur'aan?" He replied, "Of course". Sayyida Ayesha 🕮 then said, "The character of Allah's messenger 🕮 is the Qur'aan."

"Allah 🕮 commands justice and excellence, and giving to family, and He forbids vileness, evil and transgression. He urges you so that you may take heed." (Surah: Al-Nahl, Ayah no: 90)

إِنَّ اللَّهَ يَأْمُرُ بِالْعَدْلِ وَالْإِحْسَانِ وَإِيتَاءِ ذِي الْقُرْبَى وَيَنْهَى عَنِ الْفَحْشَاءِ

وَالْمُنْكَرِ وَالْبَغْيِ يَعِظُكُمْ لَعَلَّكُمْ تَذَكَّرُونَ

Mu'aadh Bin Jabal reported, "The last advice the Messenger of Allah 🕮 gave to me when I put my foot in the stirrup was that he said, "Make your character excellent for the people, O Mu'aadh Bin Jabal."

(Al-Muwatta)

Abu Darda 🕮 narrates that the Prophet 🕮 said, "Nothing will be heavier on the day of resurrection upon the scale of the believer than good character. Allah 🕮 hates one who utters foul or harsh language."

(Al-Tirmidhi)

Our Prophet Muhammad ﷺ had the best of character as Allah ﷻ confirmed in the Qur'aan. Our Prophet ﷺ informed his Ummah that the best amongst them would be the one with the best character.

This confirms to us the importance of good character and that we should all seek to develop a good character as having a good character is just as important as worshipping Allah ﷻ.

Do

- ☑ Treat everyone with respect.
- ☑ Speak nicely to everyone.
- ☑ Always help those in need.
- ☑ Behave with others how we would like them to behave with us.
- ☑ Perform noble deeds.
- ☑ Visiting the sick.
- ☑ Forgiving others.
- ☑ Making peace between others.
- ☑ Controlling anger.

Do not

- ☒ Be rude to anyone.
- ☒ Backbite or lie.
- ☒ Bully or be mean to anyone.
- ☒ Break family ties.
- ☒ Be arrogant or proud.
- ☒ Use foul language.
- ☒ Hit anyone.

Eating and drinking is very important for our health. Allah ﷻ says in the Qur'aan, "Eat and drink but do not waste; Allah ﷻ does not love those who waste".

وَكُلُوا وَاشْرَبُوا وَلَا تُسْرِفُوا إِنَّهُ لَا يُحِبُّ الْمُسْرِفِينَ

(Surah: Al-A'raf, Ayah no: 31)

By following the Sunnah habits of our Prophet Muhammad ﷺ when we eat or drink is most rewarding. To follow these mannerisms, we would be rewarded as we would if we were worshipping Allah ﷻ.

Manners of eating and drinking of the Prophet ﷺ

- The Prophet ﷺ would eat using three, occasionally four fingers. He would not eat using two fingers as He said, "That is the way Shaytaan eats."
- The Prophet ﷺ disliked eating very hot food until it had cooled down as he said, "It is without blessing; Allah ﷻ did not feed us fire, so make it cool."
- The Prophet ﷺ would lick the plate clean with His fingers and would say, "The last portion of food (on the plate) contains the most blessings."
- The Prophet ﷺ would also lick his fingers clean of food. He would say, "It is not known in which portion of the food there contains blessings."
- When the Prophet ﷺ would sit to eat, He would most often join his knees and feet together as you would when sitting in Salah, however one knee would be raised over the knee. He would say, "I am but a servant; I eat as a servant eats and sit as a servant sits."

Eating checklist

- ☑ Wash my hands before I begin to eat.
- ☑ Recite the Duaa for eating.
- ☑ Eat with my right hand using only three fingers. The thumb, index and the middle finger.
- ☑ Eat from the side of the plate nearest to me.
- ☑ Not find faults or complain about the food.
- ☑ I will not blow on my food if it is too hot but allow it to cool on its own.
- ☑ Finish all the food on my plate and lick the plate clean using my fingers.
- ☑ Lick my fingers free of food.
- ☑ Recite the Duaa after eating.
- ☑ Wash my hands after I finish eating.

Drinking checklist

- ☑ Recite Tasmiyah before drinking.
- ☑ Sit down and drink using my right hand.
- ☑ I will not drink in one go rather take 3 sips, taking a breath between each sip.
- ☑ Drink from a glass or a cup and not directly from a bottle.
- ☑ Recite Alhamdulillah (Tahmeed) when I have finished.

LESSON FIVE-WALKING

ISLAM HAS TAUGHT US THE MANNER IN WHICH EVERY ACTION SHOULD BE DONE. WE MUST WALK RESPECTFULLY IN A SIMPLE AND HUMBLE MANNER. WE SHOULD NOT WALK TOO FAST OR TOO SLOW. RATHER, WE SHOULD WALK AT A MEDIUM SPEED. THE PROPHET ﷺ WOULD WALK WITH RESPECT AND DIGNITY. HE WOULD KEEP HIS EYES ON THE PATH HE WAS WALKING ON.

I will:

- ☑ Walk on the side, not in the middle, of any street or pathway.
- ☑ Not walk with pride as Allah ﷻ dislikes those who have pride.
- ☑ Walk at a normal pace. Not too fast as though I am jogging or too slow as though I am ill.
- ☑ Lower my gaze when I am walking.
- ☑ Not stamp my feet.
- ☑ Remove anything that is harmful from the path.
- ☑ Not walk in the midst of strange men/women.
- ☑ Not walk ahead of my parents or elders.
- ☑ Be mindful of cars and other people.
- ☑ Move aside when talking to someone on the street.

EXERCISE FIVE

COMPLETE THE WORDSEARCH.

```
E  N  R  N  W  K  V  R  C  Q  P  I  Z  A  R
P  A  S  L  R  Y  U  D  E  J  E  Q  E  O  S
C  U  R  L  F  B  U  T  D  L  Z  H  P  H  U
E  E  B  G  S  A  E  Z  I  P  M  X  Z  J  C
L  J  F  S  I  M  U  Q  S  Y  Z  O  U  I  N
D  Q  H  L  C  V  U  V  T  P  J  S  P  X  C
P  P  E  F  T  I  W  J  U  Z  S  R  J  G  D
X  J  P  C  V  M  X  F  X  P  U  K  A  D  T
B  R  R  H  A  K  X  U  H  S  Q  Z  B  F  A
M  G  I  T  H  P  J  V  Q  A  E  F  G  O  Y
M  P  D  G  T  S  P  U  A  K  L  A  W  N  O
D  R  E  W  X  A  H  L  W  Z  A  N  F  U  N
P  L  W  G  Y  G  F  Y  U  D  N  L  F  F  K
R  A  L  B  Y  X  A  Z  K  Y  Y  G  V  J  Z
P  Q  J  T  F  G  K  E  L  L  R  B  V  F  T
```

Gaze	Pride
Pace	Side
Walk	Car

LESSON SIX-TALKING TO OTHERS

THE ABILITY TO SPEAK IS A GREAT BOUNTY AND BLESSING GIFTED TO US BY ALLAH ﷻ. ISLAM TEACHES US THAT WE SHOULD SPEAK OF THAT WHICH IS GOOD. WE SHOULD NOT TALK VERY LOUDLY OR TOO QUIETLY. OUR PROPHET ﷺ TAUGHT US THAT A GOOD WORD IS AN ACT OF CHARITY.

I Will:

☑ Speak about good things.

☑ Not mimic the way others speak.

☑ Look at the person who I am talking to.

☑ Make eye contact at all times.

☑ Not interrupt others when they are talking.

☑ Not shout when talking.

☑ Smile at the person I am talking to.

☑ Never lie to anyone.

☑ Not swear or use abusive language when talking.

☑ Make sure that my body faces the person I am talking to.

THE DATE PALM TREE

Sayyiduna Abdullah Ibn Umar ؓ was a companion of the Prophet ﷺ. Once, whilst he was still young, he was at a gathering with the Prophet of Allah ﷺ and his companions ؓ. The Prophet ﷺ asked his companions ؓ, "There is a tree amongst trees, the leaves of which do not wither and that is like a Muslim, tell me which tree that could be."

Everybody started to think about the trees found in the forest and Sayyiduna Abdullah Ibn Umar ؓ thought of the date-palm tree but felt hesitant to answer. After thinking about the question for some time, the companions ؓ said, "Oh Messenger of Allah ﷺ, tell us the name of this tree." The Prophet ﷺ replied "It is the date-palm tree."

Sayyiduna Abdullah Ibn Umar ؓ then narrated, "I told my father about what came to my mind." His father, Sayyiduna Umar ؓ, said, "Had you said it I would have preferred it to such and such a thing that I might possess."

PLACE A TICK NEXT TO THE ACTIONS WHICH WE SHOULD DO.

1. Use abusive language when talking ☐

2. Shout when talking ☐

3. Smile at the person one is talking to ☐

4. Never lie but speak the truth ☐

5. Make eye contact at all times ☐

لاَ يَدْخُلُ الْجَنَّةَ قَاطِعُ رَحِمٍ

"One who breaks relationships will not enter Paradise."

(Al-Bukhari)

Relatives refer to the blood-ties of a family. Allah ﷻ and his Prophet Muhammad ﷺ forbade Muslims from breaking ties with family members and have ordered Muslims to fulfil their rights.

The Prophet ﷺ said, "Giving Sadaqah to a poor person is one charity and to a relative it equals to 2 good deeds; firstly, for giving charity and secondly, for showing kindness to a relative."

Benefits of showing kindness to relatives:

- It leads to the pleasure of Allah ﷻ and his beloved Messenger ﷺ.
- Peace and harmony occurs within the society.
- Money and necessities becomes blessed.

LESSON SEVEN-VALUING YOUR TIME

TIME IS A GIFT FROM ALLAH 🕌 AND WE MUST VALUE IT. WE MUST USE IT TO ACHIEVE SUCCESS IN BOTH WORLDS. ONCE A MOMENT IN TIME HAS PASSED, IT WILL NEVER COME BACK. THE PROPHET ﷺ TAUGHT US THAT THERE ARE TWO FAVOURS GIVEN BY ALLAH 🕌, WHICH ARE FORGOTTEN BY MANY PEOPLE. THESE ARE HEALTH AND TIME.

I will:

☑ Wake up on time in the morning and pray Salah.

☑ Always sleep on time and pray Ayah Al-Kursi.

☑ Pray each Salah on time and never delay it.

☑ Do my school and Madrasah homework on time.

☑ Go to school and Madrasah ahead of time and return home straight away.

☑ Not waste my time listening to music.

☑ Use my time to serve Islam for the benefit of people.

☑ Use my time to read the Holy Qur'aan and other Islamic books.

☑ Use my time to study in Madrasah and school.

☑ Not waste my time on social media or play on my phone.

Our Prophet Muhammad ﷺ once said, "Take advantage of five matters before five other matters." They are:

1. **Your youth before you become old.** Whilst we are young, we can do many things that we will not be able to do later in life.

2. **Your health before your sickness.** We should thank Allah ﷻ for good health and spend our time worshipping Allah ﷻ. If we fall ill and cannot do the same good deeds as we did when we were healthy then Allah ﷻ will still grant us the same reward.

3. **Your wealth before your poverty.** We should be very careful in spending our money on things that benefit us. Wasting money is the way of Shaytaan.

4. **Your free time before you become busy.** On the Day of Judgement, we will be questioned on how we spent our time.

5. **Your life before your death.** We cannot change anything about our life after it comes to an end. We must spend our life doing things that will benefit us and others.

MATCH EACH ITEM ON THE LEFT WITH EACH ITEM ON THE RIGHT.

Wealth before poverty

Life before death

Youth before old age

Health before sickness

Time before you are busy

LESSON EIGHT-GIVING GIFTS

GIVING GIFTS IS THE SUNNAH OF OUR PROPHET ﷺ. WE SHOULD GIVE A GIFT TO OUR PARENTS, RELATIVES, NEIGHBOURS AND OTHER FRIENDS AS IT CREATES LOVE AND AFFECTION BETWEEN US. WE SHOULD ALWAYS THANK ONE ANOTHER BY SAYING JAZAKALLAH KHAYRAN.

1. Giving and accepting gifts is a Sunnah.

2. We should try to give more in return.

3. Give gifts for the sake of Allah ﷻ.

4. We should not reject a gift from anyone.

5. We should not gift anything which is not allowed in Islam.

6. We should try to give Islamic gifts, especially books of knowledge, to promote learning of our religion.

The Prophet Muhammad's ﷺ Guidance

- Whoever does you a favour then reward him, if you cannot reward him then pray for him/her.

- The Messenger of Allah ﷺ would accept gifts and would give something in return.

- In order to promote love, exchange gifts amongst yourselves.

- Exchange presents with one another. Presents remove evil from hearts.

IMAM ABU HANIFA ﷺ AND THE GIFT

Once, a man brought Imam Abu Hanifa ﷺ a gift worth ten dirhams. In return, the Imam presented him a gift worth five hundred dirhams. The man was surprised and said, "But Imam, my gift was little, about a tenth of your gift!"

The Imaam answered, "Your gift is more valuable as you remembered me whilst I had forgotten you. I remembered you only after you had given me your gift. This is why your gift is better."

> **IF SOMEONE OFFERS US A GIFT, WE SHOULD ACCEPT IT EVEN IF IT IS LITTLE. ALWAYS TRY AND GIVE SOMETHING BETTER IN RETURN.**

ANSWER THE FOLLOWING QUESTIONS.

1. For whose sake should we gift others?

    _____

2. Is it Fardh, Sunnah or Mustahab to give and receive gifts?

    _____

3. Should we try to give more in return? State Yes or No.

    _____

4. If you cannot reward someone for a favour, what should you do?

    _____

5. State one thing you have learnt from the Prophet's ﷺ guidance.

    _____

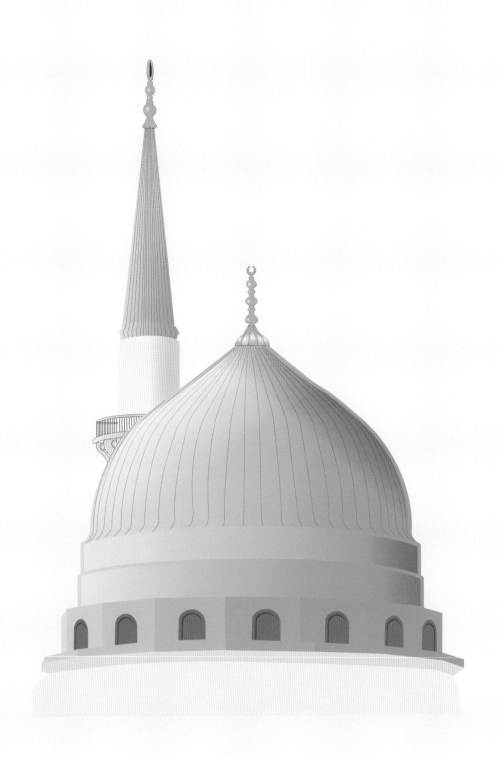

LESSON NINE-HONOURING OUR NEIGHBOURS

ISLAM IS A RELIGION OF PEACE. IT TEACHES US TO TREAT OUR NEIGHBOURS KINDLY AND FAIRLY. THE MESSENGER OF ALLAH SAID, "ANYONE WHO BELIEVES IN ALLAH AND THE DAY OF JUDGEMENT SHOULD HONOUR HIS NEIGHBOUR." HE ALSO SAID, "THE BEST NEIGHBOUR IS ONE WHO BEHAVES BEST TOWARDS HIS NEIGHBOURS."

I Will:

☑ Help my neighbours when they are in need of help.

☑ Not trouble my neighbours.

☑ Share good food with my neighbours.

☑ Visit my neighbours when they are ill or suffering.

☑ Protect my neighbours from harm or injury.

☑ Not speak ill of my neighbours, even if they treat us badly.

☑ Protect my neighbours' home when they are away.

Our Prophet Muhammad's Guidance

"He is not a believer whose stomach is filled while the neighbour to his side goes hungry."

MALIK BIN DINAR AND HIS NEIGHBOUR

Malik Bin Dinar رحمه الله rented a house. His neighbour was Jewish and Malik Bin Dinar's رحمه الله room was near the door of the neighbour. His neighbour would throw his waste into the house of Malik Bin Dinar رحمه الله. He did this for some time but Malik Bin Dinar رحمه الله said nothing.

One day his neighbour asked, "Do you not suffer from my throwing the rubbish?"

He replied, "Yes I do, but I clean it up"

His neighbour said, "Do you not get angry?"

Malik Bin Dinar رحمه الله then said, "My lord teaches us in the Qur'aan that we should restrain anger and forgive people."

After hearing this, his neighbour's heart became soft and he said, "Without doubt your religion is good. Today I accept Islam with all my heart."

> **GOOD BEHAVIOUR IS ALWAYS BENEFICIAL AND LEADS TO GOODNESS.**

EXERCISE NINE

FILL IN THE GAPS USING THE WORDS IN THE BOXES BELOW.

Speak   Share   Harm

Ill   Protect   Badly

1. I will protect my neighbours from _____ and injury.

2. I will _____ my neighbours' home when they are away.

3. I will not _____ ill of my neighbours.

4. I will _____ good food with my neighbours.

5. I will visit my neighbours when they are _____ or suffering. Even if they treat us _____.